J.K. LASSER'S ™

Gay Finances in a Straight World

J.K. LASSER'S ™

Gay Finances in a Straight World

A Comprehensive Financial Planning Handbook

**Peter M. Berkery, Jr.
and Gregory A. Diggins**

MACMILLAN • USA

MACMILLAN GENERAL REFERENCE
A Simon & Schuster Macmillan Company
1633 Broadway
New York, NY 10019-6785

Macmillan Publishing books may be purchased for business or sales promotional use. For information please write: Special Markets Department, Macmillan Publishing USA, 1633 Broadway, New York, NY 10019-6785.

J.K. Lasser Editorial and Production
Elliott Eiss, Member of the New York Bar, Editorial Director of the J.K. Lasser Institute™
Maryam Banikarim, Publisher
Connor Murphy, Senior Contributing Editor
John Hunt, Graphic Coordinator
Paul Costello, Cover Design
Claire Smith, Marketing
Nick Petro, Manufacturing
Helen Chin, Production Editor

International Standard Book Number: ISBN 0-02-862222-7
Library of Congress Cataloging-in-Publication Data: 97-80929

Manufactured in the United States of America

10 9 8 7 6 5 4 3 2 1

Design by designLab, Seattle

Contents

Table of Selected Worksheets, Checklists, and Charts

Introduction

THE FINANCIAL PLANNING PROCESS

Most professionals counsel their clients to think of financial planning as a *process* (as opposed to a one-time event). There are several ways to describe this process. Because this book is intended to provide a hands-on and results-oriented focus, it uses the following approach to the financial planning process:

1. Identify your financial goals.

2. Establish dollar amounts for achieving your goals.

3. Implement appropriate investment strategies for achieving your goals.

4. Protect against the obstacles that could keep you from achieving your goals through the use of:

   a. Insurance planning

   b. Estate planning

   c. Income tax planning

   d. Incapacity planning

5. Periodically review both the progress you've made toward achieving your goals and the strategies you've implemented to avoid the obstacles along the way.

Most importantly, the book identifies the strategies lesbians and gay men—and particularly couples—need in order to use the financial planning process successfully.

What's Different for Lesbians and Gay Men?

Although lesbians and gay men no doubt share the financial goals common to all Americans, it is perhaps surprising but certainly true that the strategies for reaching those goals can be markedly different. There are a number of possible factors contributing to this:

1. For couples, the legal barrier to marriage creates dozens (if not hundreds) of inequities that must be planned for, planned around, or otherwise addressed.

2. Even where the legal barrier to marriage is not directly at issue, many of the products and services used in the financial planning process simply have not been designed with lesbian and gay couples in mind (auto insurance, some retirement plans).

3. For lesbians and gay men geographically or emotionally isolated from their families, the support system presumed in several areas of financial planning (retirement planning, disability planning) may not exist.

4. For some in the community, the specter of AIDS has caused a sense of hopelessness regarding the likelihood of growing old, and with it the need to plan for the future.

5. For those directly affected by HIV, the formidable financial consequences of living with the virus create a unique and acute set of needs.

6. For others in the community, the promising results obtained from emerging drug therapies are causing a shift in focus toward long-term goals for the first time.

7. Modern culture in general, and gay culture in particular, are youth-oriented, creating attitudinal barriers toward planning for old age.

8. As part of the coming out process, some gay men and lesbians come to view the products and services used in the financial planning process as something only straight people need to think about—

much like the minivan and the white picket fence. This, too, can create attitudinal barriers toward the financial planning process.

9. Some lesbians and gay men view the financial institutions closely associated with financial planning as traditionally indifferent or even homophobic, creating mistrust with regard to the products and services they offer.

Throughout this book, the issues these considerations can raise are integrated into an action-oriented explanation of the financial planning process, ensuring that the strategies you employ will enable you to protect and achieve your goals.

PART I

Getting Started:
Financial Planning Fundamentals

CHAPTER 1

Setting Financial Goals

Regardless of who you are or where you are in life, the financial planning process is about setting and achieving goals. While your goals will require money, they shouldn't be *about* money. Instead, they should be about what money can enable you to do. Your goals should reflect what's important in your life and what you think will bring you happiness and satisfaction—in the words of Joseph Campbell, what will allow you to "follow your bliss."

With this in mind, take a moment right now to shut your eyes and think about your life goals. Where do you see yourself in ten years? Twenty years? What will you be doing? What will your partner be doing? These really are hard questions, and it's not always easy to set goals. While financial planning can tell you how to get to where you want to be, it can't tell you where to go—that's for you to decide.

The checklist below contains many of the goals people commonly hope to achieve through the financial planning process. It may help you in thinking about your own goals. Don't feel constrained by the checklist, though; your goals should be limited only by your own imagination. If you need to add a goal or two at the bottom, do so.

FIGURE 1-1
SETTING FINANCIAL GOALS.

Use the checklist below to identify those financial goals important to you. Also identify the goals for which you already have a plan in place.

Goal	Important to Me	In Place
Establish an emergency fund	____	____
Buy a _____	____	____
Buy a vacation house or a boat	____	____
Go to—or go back to—school	____	____
Start a business	____	____
Start a family	____	____
Take a major vacation	____	____
Be financially secure in retirement	____	____
_____	____	____
_____	____	____

Now, review your list of goals and identify the two or three most important to you at this stage in your life for which you don't yet have a plan in place. It's hard to plan for more than a few goals simultaneously, so try to set some priorities and avoid going over three goals. As you work through this book, keep these goals in mind; refer back to them, and apply what you read to implement strategies for achieving them. By the end of the book, you should have a firm understanding of how to reach each of the goals you've set.

If you're in a relationship, you might want to share your goals with your partner. Does he or she have similar goals? Should you plan for them together or individually? What goals are important to him or her, and where do they fit in your planning? Again, these are genuinely challenging questions, but you'll want to address them before you get too far into the process, since the answers will affect your planning decisions.

Once you've identified your goals, you need to quantify them. That is, you need to assign dollar values and time frames to each one. It's nearly impossible to achieve your goals unless you do this. Goals like "becoming rich" or "retiring young" mean different things to different people. You have a much better chance of becoming rich or retiring young if you state your goal as "saving $1 million by age 50." Thus, some of the other goals suggested in the checklist above might be quantified as "buy a $25,000 sailboat in five years," or "save $50,000 to start my own business in three years." Setting goals in this manner allows you to understand what will be required to actually reach them.

Once you've set your goals, it's time to learn how to achieve them. The rest of this book is designed to help you understand the many complex rules, products, services, risks, and rewards you will face as you design and implement strategies for achieving your goals.

CHAPTER 2

Taking Stock: Computing Your Net Worth

I n order to determine how to reach your financial goals, you must first understand your current financial situation. One of the tools that can help you do so is called a *balance sheet*. The balance sheet provides an orderly presentation of your *assets* (what you own) and your *liabilities* (what you owe). The difference between the two is referred to as your *net worth* (i.e., assets – liabilities = net worth). Your net worth is a fundamental representation of your current financial position, and is essential to many aspects of the planning process.

To make the best use of the information that will be in your balance sheet, you should divide your assets into three categories:

1. Cash or cash equivalents

2. Invested assets

3. Use assets

The three tables below will help you understand which assets belong in each category. Use these tables to help you make a complete inventory of all your assets.

FIGURE 2-1
CASH AND CASH EQUIVALENTS

Type of Asset	Examples
Cash	Money in your pocket, in a safe, stored around the house
Checking Accounts	A bank, credit union, or brokerage account
Savings Accounts	A bank, credit union, or brokerage account
Money Markets	A bank, credit union, brokerage house, or mutual fund account
Certificates of Deposit	CDs issued by a bank or credit union
Life Insurance	The cash value accumulated in the policy (not the death benefit)

FIGURE 2-2
INVESTED ASSETS

Type of Asset	Examples
U.S. Securities	EE bonds, HH bonds, 90-day treasury bills, 30-year treasury bonds
Government Bonds	Municipal bonds, highway bonds
Corporate Debt	Bonds of U.S. companies, bonds of foreign companies
Corporate Equity	Common stock, preferred stock, foreign stock
Mutual Funds	Stock funds, bond funds, index funds (don't list retirement funds here)
Real Estate	Rental property, raw land (don't list residences here)
Small Businesses	Any partnership, limited liability company, sole proprietorship, S corporation you own and run
Retirement Plans	Individual Retirement Accounts (IRAs), 401(k) plans, 403(b) plans
Other Investments	Gold, precious metals, stock futures or options

FIGURE 2-3
USE ASSETS

Type of Asset	Examples
Residences	Main home, vacation home
Vehicles	Cars, campers, boats
Personal Property	Household furnishings, china, crystal, silverware, clothing, jewelry, furs
Artwork/Collectibles	Valuable artwork, rugs, antiques, coin, stamp, or book collections

Once you've identified and categorized all your assets, you'll need to go through a similar exercise for your liabilities. Although liabilities aren't divided into categories the way assets are, you'll still want to use the following table to be sure you've identified all of yours.

FIGURE 2-4
LIABILITIES

Type of Liability	Examples
Credit Cards	Bank, retail, oil company credit cards
Vehicle Loans	Car loan, boat loan
Student Loans	SallieMae loan, bank loan, PLUS loan
Other Loans	Nonsecured bank loan, line of credit
Mortgages	First mortgage, second mortgage, home equity line
Other Loans	Money owed to your business, family, or friends

Once you have identified all your assets and liabilities, you are ready to create your balance sheet. Take a look at the sample balance sheet below for I. M. Outthere. Then, use your list of assets and liabilities to complete the blank balance sheet provided.

Lesbian and gay couples will need to decide whether to prepare separate balance sheets or a combined balance sheet. If you and your partner keep your finances completely separate, then separate statements would be more appropriate. Similarly, if you are planning for individual goals, then individual balance sheets would be more useful. If you do prepare separate balance sheets, be sure to list only each partner's individual share of joint assets and liabilities.

Figure 2-5
SAMPLE BALANCE SHEET

I. M. OUTTHERE
Balance Sheet
as of December 31, 19XX

Assets		Liabilities and Net Worth	
Cash and Cash Equivalent		**Liabilities**	
Cash on hand	$ 100	Credit cards	$ 10,000
Checking account	1,000	Vehicle loan	15,000
Money Market	20,000	Student loan	22,600
Cash Value of		Mortgage	195,000
Life Insurance	3,000		
Total Cash and		Total Liabilities	$242,600
Cash Equivalents	$24,100		
Invested Assets			
Stocks	$10,000		
EE Savings Bonds	2,000		
Mutual Funds	15,000		
IRAs	12,500		
401(k)	30,000		
Total Invested Assets	$69,500		
Use Assets		Net Worth	214,400
Condominium	$175,000		
Beach House	125,000		
Vehicles	23,000		
Personal Property	40,400		
Total Use Assets	$363,400		
		Total Liabilities	
Total Assets	$457,000	and Net Worth	$457,000

Figure 2-6
YOUR BALANCE SHEET

Balance Sheet As
of December 31, 19XX

Assets		Liabilities and Net Worth	
Cash and Cash Equivalents		Liabilities	
Cash on hand	$ _____	Credit cards	$ _____
Checking account	_____	Vehicle loan	_____
Savings Account	_____	Mortgage	_____
Cash Value of Life	_____		_____
Insurance Plans	_____		_____
_____	_____		
_____	_____	Total Liabilities	$ _____
Total Cash and Cash Equivalents	$ _____		
Invested Assets			
Stocks	$ _____		
Mutual Funds	_____		
Retirement Plans	_____		
_____	_____		
_____	_____		
_____	_____		
Total Invested Assets	$ _____		
Use Assets		Net Worth	$ _____
House	$ _____		
Vehicles	_____		
Personal Property	_____		
	_____		
	_____		
Total Use Assets	$ _____		
		Total Liabilities	
Total Use Assets	$ _____	and Net Worth	$ _____

INTERPRETING YOUR BALANCE SHEET

Now that you've prepared your balance sheet, consider the following ways to put it to work for you:

Monitoring Progress. It takes time to reach financial goals. Short-term goals, such as saving for a down payment on a house or for a vacation, are more readily attained. Long-term goals, like saving for retirement or a child's education, will require monitoring. Preparing an annual balance sheet is one way to measure your progress towards reaching your goals.

Emergency Fund. An adequate emergency fund is an important financial goal for everybody. It allows you to respond to a sudden need for cash (e.g., job loss, temporary disability, major home repair) without having to tap into invested assets or borrow on high-interest credit cards. You should have a ready cash reserve sufficient to cover your living expenses for at least three and up to six months. You can use your balance sheet to identify those sources of cash.

Insurance Planning. The balance sheet provides useful information for several aspects of insurance planning. First, by comparing asset values on your balance sheet against the amounts listed on your insurance policies, you can determine whether or not you have adequate property coverage. For example, if your home's value is $175,000 but your policy is for the original purchase price of $150,000, you will need to update your insurance for inflation. Next, if your balance sheet indicates that you own valuables over the amounts covered by your basic property coverage, then you may need a separate rider to cover these items. Finally, your balance sheet can help you decide whether or not you need life insurance. If you have large liabilities that could not be paid in the event of an untimely death, life insurance coverage would be an effective way to plan for this risk.

Investment Planning. Your balance sheet can give you a rough sense of whether your investment portfolio is properly diversified. The invested assets section shows how your portfolio is currently allocated among the various types of investments. For example, if you have $50,000 in cash, and only $5,000 in invested assets, it's likely your portfolio needs to be reallocated.

Estate Planning. Because it lists all of your assets, the balance sheet can help you decide what to leave to whom when you die. Moreover, the net worth reported on your balance sheet is the starting point for determining whether you need to be concerned about the federal estate tax. If your net worth (or the combined net worth of yourself and your partner if you are in a relationship) is above or near $625,000, it is likely you will need to do some estate tax planning.

CHAPTER 3

Building a Budget

A *cash flow statement* summarizes your historical income and expenses over a one-year period. It is a blueprint for where your money came from and where it went. A *budget* is similar to a cash flow statement, except it is an attempt to project income and expenses looking *forward* for one year instead of backward. Your budget will help you understand and control where your money goes. You can use your prior year's cash flow statement as the basis for building your current year's budget. At the end of the year, you also can compare your budget to your cash flow statement to see how well your projections matched up to your actual experience.

Although the process for creating both the cash flow statement and the budget is the same, the budget tends to be a more helpful planning tool. A budget is divided into two main parts: *inflows* and *outflows*. Outflows are further broken down into three subcategories: (1) savings and investments; (2) fixed outflows; and (3) variable outflows. Use the tables below to help you understand and identify your financial inflows and outflows.

FIGURE 3-1
INFLOWS

Type of Inflow	Examples
Wages and salaries	Gross pay, net earnings from a sole proprietorship or partnership
Interest	Bank interest, interest on government bonds
Dividends	Stock dividends, mutual fund dividends
Other income	Gifts or inheritances, pensions, Social Security, other government benefits

FIGURE 3-2
OUTFLOWS

Type of Outflow	Examples
Savings and Investment	401(k) contributions, systematic mutual fund purchases, direct deposit to savings
Fixed Outflows	
Housing expense	Mortgage or rent payment, property taxes (do not include repairs here)
Vehicle expense	Loan or lease payments (do not include operating expenses here)
Other debts	Credit card payments, student loans, bank loans, loans from family or friends
Insurance premiums	Payments on life, health, disability, homeowners, and automobile policies
Variable Outflows	
Income Taxes	Federal, state, and local income taxes, Social Security and Medicare taxes
Food	Groceries and dining out
Transportation	Gasoline, oil, parking, tolls, repairs, car washes, and public transportation
Clothing	Clothing purchases, dry cleaning, alterations

continues

(continued)

Type of Outflow	Examples
Entertainment/vacations	Travel, movies, plays, books, recordings, club dues
Health care	Insurance deductibles, expenses not covered by health insurance
Utilities/household	Water, gas, electric, telephone, cable television, household repairs and supplies, cleaning services, yard care
Contributions	Donations to church, temple and other tax-exempt organizations
Other expenses	Education expenses, child care, pet care, pocket money

Note that if you have an "other expense" that is high, you should create a separate line for it under your variable outflows. This will help you better track and manage your expenses.

Once you have identified your inflows and outflows, you can prepare your budget. First take a look at the personal budget for I. M. Outthere, and then use the blank to prepare your own. If you're in a relationship, you'll probably want to prepare a combined budget, unless you and your partner maintain separate finances. If you do prepare separate budgets, be sure you only include each partner's share of joint income or expenses in each budget.

Figure 3-3
Sample Budget

I. M. OUTTHERE
PERSONAL BUDGET FOR
THE YEAR ENDING DECEMBER 31, 19XX

Inflows	Annually	Monthly
Wages and Salaries	$62,640	$5,220
Interest	1,200	100
Dividends	600	50
Other	300	25
Total Inflows	$64,740	$5,395
Outflows		
Savings and Investments	$ 6,000	$ 500
Fixed Outflows:		
Housing Expenses	18,000	1,500
Vehicle Expenses	4,800	400
Other Debts	6,000	500
Insurance Premiums	900	75
Total Fixed Outflows	$29,700	$2,475
Variable Outflows:		
Taxes	12,000	1,000
Food	4,800	400
Transportation	1,200	100
Clothing	1,200	100
Entertainment and Vacations	3,000	250
Health Care	2,400	200
Utilities/Household Expenses	1,800	150
Charitable Contributions	1,800	150
Other Expenses	840	70
Total Variable Outflows	29,040	2,420
Total Outflows	$64,740	$5,395

Figure 3-4
Your Budget

PERSONAL BUDGET FOR
THE YEAR ENDING DECEMBER 31, 19XX

<u>Inflows</u>	<u>Annually</u>	<u>Monthly</u>
Wages and Salaries	$ _____	$ _____
Interest	_____	_____
Dividends	_____	_____
Other	_____	_____
Total Inflows	$ _____	$ _____
<u>Outflows</u>		
Savings and Investments	$ _____	$ _____
Fixed Outflows:		
Housing Expenses	_____	_____
Vehicle Expenses	_____	_____
Other Debts	_____	_____
Insurance Premiums	_____	_____
Total Fixed Outflows	_____	_____
Variable Outflows:		
Taxes	_____	_____
Food	_____	_____
Transportation	_____	_____
Clothing	_____	_____
Entertainment and Vacations	_____	_____
Health Care	_____	_____
Utilities/Household Expenses	_____	_____
Charitable Contributions	_____	_____
_____	_____	_____
Other Expenses	_____	_____
Total Variable Outflows	_____	_____
Total Outflows	$ _____	$ _____

USING YOUR BUDGET

Just like your balance sheet, your budget is a critical financial planning tool. It enables you to identify the resources available to meet your financial goals, and to make informed choices about your financial priorities.

Making Ends Meet. Your budget is balanced if your inflows equal your outflows. Thus, if you have a surplus in your budget, allocate the extra to savings and investment. If your budget is not balanced, one of your first financial planning goals must be to bring it into balance. To do this, start by trying to identify expenses you can cut within your variable outflows. Are you eating out too often? Are you spending money for a health club membership you don't use? As unpleasant as it is to contemplate, you must do whatever is necessary to regain financial balance. If your budget still is not balanced after adjusting your variable outflows, you will have to take a look at fixed outflows. Here, the choices are even more difficult. You may have to consider finding a roommate, or moving to a smaller place. Carpool or take public transportation to work. If you have considerable credit card debt but a clean credit history, try to negotiate a lower interest rate. If your budget is still out of balance after you've done everything possible to your variable and fixed outflows, you should seek the advice of a nonprofit credit counseling service.

Paying Savings First. Even though your budget needs to balance, it's unlikely you will meet your financial goals just by having your inflows match your outflows. You'll have to focus on ways to increase your outflows to savings and investment—that's why they have their own line in your budget! Once you get into the habit of "paying savings first," you will be on your way to meeting your financial goals. One easy way to do this is to set up automatic deposits to savings or through payroll withholding or other electronic transfer. If your employer has a 401(k) plan, sign up. Send money directly to your broker or mutual fund company on a monthly basis. Once you've set up an automatic savings mechanism, try to increase the amount you save as your income increases. You'll be amazed at how you don't even miss the money if you never even "see" it!

PART II

Crunching the Numbers: Determining How Much to Save

CHAPTER 4

Saving for Basic Financial Goals

"How much do I need to save to reach my goal?"

It's a question at the heart of much of financial planning. It's an important question, and it can be a difficult one, too, because there are a number of different variables that must be taken into account. How long is the time frame you've set for achieving your goal? What rate of return will your savings earn along the way? What impact will inflation have on the amount of money you need?

As these questions imply, computing the amount you'll need to save to reach a financial goal can involve some complex number-crunching. That's why people who are saving for major goals—like starting a business or retiring—often call in outside help. This help can come in the form of a financial planning professional, a computer software program, or some combination of the two. People who consult with an advisor in these circumstances usually find that their time and money have been well-spent.

Nevertheless, there will be times when you'll want to take a stab at crunching the numbers yourself. Your goal may be modest, your resources may be limited, or you may only want a rough idea of how the process works and what its results mean for you.

The worksheet in the figure below and the line-by-line instructions that follow it will give you this rough idea. Although it can be a helpful tool in understanding what is required to reach a financial goal, you should use it with caution. In particular, keep the following in mind:

1. The process involves several variables. A change in even one variable is likely to produce a dramatic change in the end result.

2. In order to simplify the worksheet, a single assumption regarding inflation rates—i.e., 3.5 percent—was used. While this is a responsible assumption, be aware that actual inflation rates higher or lower than 3.5 percent will have an impact on your result. If long-term inflation is higher than 3.5 percent, you'll need more than you've projected; if it is lower, you'll need less.

3. The line-by-line instructions following the worksheet contain several tables providing dollar amounts to be entered on the worksheet. These dollar amounts have been rounded in order to make them easier to work with. A special rounding convention was used to ensure that you get appropriate results. In other words, instead of rounding up for five and above, the tables round up more conservatively. This should help ensure reliable savings estimates. However, bear in mind that whenever figures are rounded, a small margin of error arises.

4. This worksheet should be used only for basic financial goals, such as saving to buy a house, start a business, or fund education expenses. Some financial goals entail even more complex calculations. In particular, several additional steps are required to compute retirement savings needs; because retirement planning is such an important and universal financial planning goal, it is covered separately in the next chapter.

After you've studied the worksheet and the instructions, be sure to review the illustrations that follow to get a better understanding of how to compute your monthly savings needs.

FIGURE 4-1
MONTHLY SAVINGS WORKSHEET
FOR BASIC FINANCIAL GOALS

1. Total Needed for Goal (in Today's Dollars) $ _____

2. Amount Already Saved for Goal $ _____

3. Additional Amount Needed for Goal
   (in Today's Dollars [Line 1 –Line 2]) $ _____

4. Additional Amount Needed for Goal
   (in Future Dollars [from Line 3 and Figure 4-2]) $ _____

5. Total Monthly Savings Requirement for Goal

   A. Monthly Savings Amount per Thousand (from Figure 4-3) $ _____

   B. Thousands Needed (from Line 4) $ _____

   C. Total Monthly Savings Required (Line 5A × Line 5B) $ _____

6. Additional Monthly Savings Requirement for Goal

   A. Current Monthly Savings for Goal $ _____

   B. Additional Monthly Savings Required
      for Goal (Line 5C – Line 6A) $ _____

Line 1. Enter the total amount you anticipate you'll need for your goal on Line 1. Because it's difficult to predict expenses in the future, it's best to begin by thinking about what your goal would cost in today's dollars. Later in the worksheet, you'll "grow" your needs into future dollars to account for inflation.

Line 2. If you've already set aside money you know will be available for your goal, enter it on Line 2.

Line 3. Subtract Line 2 from Line 1 to determine the additional amount you'll need to save in order to achieve your goal.

Line 4. You must estimate what your additional savings amount will need to be at the end of the timeframe you've established for your goal. In other words, you'll need to "grow" the amount for the inflation likely to occur between now and the time you plan to achieve your goal. Use the table below to find how much your savings goal will need to be at the end of your timeframe, and enter that amount on Line 4.

FIGURE 4-2
INFLATING YOUR GOAL

Savings In Today's Dollars	Years to Achieve Goal					
	3	5	7	10	15	20
10,000	11,100	11,900	12,800	14,100	16,700	19,900
15,000	16,600	17,800	19,100	21,200	25,100	29,900
20,000	22,200	23,800	25,500	28,200	33,500	39,800
25,000	27,700	29,700	31,800	35,300	41,900	49,800
30,000	33,300	35,600	38,200	42,300	50,300	59,700
40,000	44,400	47,500	50,900	56,200	67,000	79,600
50,000	55,500	59,400	63,600	70,500	83,800	99,500
75,000	83,200	89,100	95,400	105,800	125,700	149,300
100,000	110,900	118,800	127,200	141,100	167,600	199,000

Line 5A. Once you've established the total amount you'll need at the end of your time frame to achieve your goal, you must determine how much to save each month in order to get there. This computation requires several steps. On Line 5A, enter the amount from table 4-3 below that corresponds to the number of years you've set to achieve your goal and the investment return you expect your savings to earn along the way.

Note that in order to use table 4-3, you must assume a rate of investment return for your monthly savings. The money you save each month will be invested until you reach your goal. Regardless of whether you invest your monthly savings in a bank account, a mutual fund, or cattle futures, you will have to make an assumption about the rate of return that it will earn. Your assumption will be a product of two factors: your risk tolerance and your time frame.

FIGURE 4-3
MONTHLY SAVINGS REQUIRED PER $1,000

Assumed Rate of Return	Years to Achieve Goal					
	3	**5**	**7**	**10**	**15**	**20**
4%	26.20	15.10	10.40	6.80	4.10	2.80
5%	25.80	14.70	10.00	6.50	3.80	2.50
6%	25.50	14.40	9.60	6.10	3.50	2.20
7%	25.10	14.00	9.30	5.80	3.20	2.00
8%	24.70	13.60	9.00	5.50	2.90	1.70
9%	24.30	13.30	8.60	5.20	2.70	1.50
10%	24.00	13.00	8.30	4.90	2.50	1.40
11%	23.60	12.60	8.00	4.60	2.20	1.20
12%	23.30	12.30	7.70	4.40	2.00	1.00

Chapter 6 of this book is devoted to understanding risk and risk tolerance, as well as the relation of the two to an investment's rate of return. It even includes a short quiz to help you assess your risk tolerance. It might be helpful to review that material before attempting this part of the worksheet. However, if you want to complete a rough assessment of your monthly savings needs quickly, and are willing to accept a rule of thumb, the table below can help. Locate your risk tolerance and time frame on the table, and use the corresponding rate of return in working with Figure 4-3 above.

FIGURE 4-4
RATE OF RETURN ASSUMPTIONS—A ROUGH GUIDE

Your Risk Tolerance	Your Time Frame		
	Short (3–5 Years)	Medium (5–10 Years)	Long (10+ Years)
Low	4%	6%	8%
Average	6%	8%	10%
High	8%	10%	12%

If you feel that your risk tolerance falls somewhere in between "low" and "average" or in between "average" and "high," use a rate of return assumption between those suggested in the table above. Also, keep in mind that actual results that deviate from your assumed rate of return are likely to have a profound impact on your ability to achieve your goal; make your assumptions carefully!

Line 5B. The information you computed for Line 5A only tells you how much you need to save for $1,000. Now you have to multiply that amount by the number of thousands in your goal. For example, if your goal (from Line 4) is $50,000, you would enter 50 on Line 5B; if your goal was $75,000, you would enter 75 on Line 5B; and so on.

Line 5C. To compute your total monthly savings requirement, multiply the monthly savings amount per thousand (Line 5A) by the number of thousands needed to reach your goal (Line 5B).

Line 6A. If you're already setting aside an amount each month toward your goal, and you plan to continue setting this amount aside each month, enter it on Line 6A. If you're not currently saving anything toward your goal, enter "0".

Line 6B. Subtract the amount on Line 6A from the amount on Line 5C to determine the additional amount you'll need to save each month in order to achieve your financial goal.

ILLUSTRATION

Max wants to buy a house in five years. He estimates he will need $30,000 for the down payment and closing costs. He currently sets aside $150 per month toward the house, and already has saved $5,000 toward his goal. Max considers his risk tolerance to be average, and therefore assumes a 7 percent rate of return on his savings.

FIGURE 4-5
MAX'S MONTHLY SAVINGS WORKSHEET

1. Total Needed for Goal (in Today's Dollars)	$30,000
2. Amount Already Saved for Goal	$5,000
3. Additional Amount Needed for Goal (in Today's Dollars [Line 1 – Line 2])	$25,000
4. Additional Amount Needed for Goal (in Future Dollars [from Line 3 and Figure 4-2])	$29,700
5. Total Monthly Savings Requirement for Goal	
A. Monthly Savings Amount per Thousand (from Figure 4-3)	$14
B. Thousands Needed (from Line 4)	30
C. Total Monthly Savings Required (Line 5A × Line 5B)	$420
6. Additional Monthly Savings Requirement for Goal	
A. Current Monthly Savings for Goal	$150
B. Additional Monthly Savings Required for Goal (Line 5C – Line 6A)	$270

ILLUSTRATION

Germaine wants to quit her job in ten years to start her own business. She estimates she will need $100,000 to start the business and maintain her personal cash flow until the business is viable. She currently is not saving toward this goal. Because of the time frame involved, Germaine decides her risk tolerance is high, and that she will be able to invest her savings to achieve a 12 percent rate of return.

FIGURE 4-6
GERMAINE'S MONTHLY SAVINGS WORKSHEET

1. Total Needed for Goal (in Today's Dollars)	$100,000
2. Amount Already Saved for Goal	0
3. Additional Amount Needed for Goal (in Today's Dollars [Line 1 – Line 2])	$100,000
4. Additional Amount Needed for Goal (in Future Dollars [from Line 3 and Figure 4-2])	$141,100
5. Total Monthly Savings Requirement for Goal	
A. Monthly Savings Amount per Thousand (from Figure 4-3)	$4.40
B. Thousands Needed (from Line 4)	141
C. Total Monthly Savings Required (Line 5A × Line 5B)	$620
6. Additional Monthly Savings Requirement for Goal	
A. Current Monthly Savings for Goal	0
B. Additional Monthly Savings Required for Goal (Line 5C – Line 6A)	$620

A quick word about the impact of taxes on your savings: the numbers you crunched in this chapter did not take into account any taxes you would owe on the interest, dividends, and capital gains your savings will earn as it grows toward achieving your goal. Therefore, the money to pay those taxes will have to come from other sources, and not from the savings itself. Strategies for deferring and minimizing the impact of taxes on your savings and investing are discussed in chapter 17.

What If It Doesn't Work?

What happens if you've gone through the worksheet, and you can't achieve your goal within your time frame given your risk tolerance? People tend to gloss over this important question because it's unpleasant—but it happens. Simply put, the answer is that one of the variables must be changed. You either have to adjust the amount of your goal, lengthen your time frame, or increase your risk tolerance in order to earn a higher rate of return.

You are 45 years old. Your goal is to save $100,000 so you and your partner can take a cruise around the world when you are 60. You can afford to invest $250 per month toward this goal. However, you project that, given your risk tolerance and time frame, you only will be able to save $85,000, leaving you $15,000 short of your goal.

Option 1. After discussing it with your partner, you decide it will be possible to alter your itinerary and accomplish your goal with the lower amount.

Option 2. After discussing it with your partner, you conclude that you will need the full $100,000 if this is to be the trip of a lifetime. You decide to increase your monthly investment from $250 to $300 by reallocating $50 from the monthly entertainment/vacation expenditures in your current budget in order to reach your goal.

Option 3. Instead, you and your partner decide to alter your time frame and defer your trip to age 62 in order to reach your goal.

Option 4. You and your partner conclude that if you accept slightly more investment risk, you can meet your $100,000 goal by age 60 and investing only $250 per month.

Note that, of all the variables you can change to achieve your goal, adjusting your risk tolerance (as in Option 4) will be the hardest. Attitudes toward risk are fundamental personality traits, and, by the time you're old enough to be setting financial goals, they're pretty well set. Perhaps by keeping an eye on a long time frame you can expand the edges of your tolerance, but you should not expect to make fundamental changes in your approach to risk. Moreover, you should be very hesitant about dealing with a financial planning professional who attempts to push you too hard in this direction. Again, risk and risk tolerance are explored in detail later in the book.

CHAPTER 5

Saving for Retirement

"How much should I be saving each month for retirement?"

One of the most important financial goals people set for themselves is saving for a secure retirement. It also is one of the most difficult goals to quantify, much more so than basic financial goals. There are several reasons for this: the time frames involved are longer, making projections more uncertain; the ultimate goal is not so much to save a lump-sum of money in and of itself, but to save a lump-sum that will generate a desired income stream throughout retirement; other possible sources of retirement income (an employer pension, Social Security) may need to be taken into consideration; and, all the concerns regarding assumptions made—inflation, rates of return—discussed in the last chapter apply here.

If the number-crunching in the last chapter was difficult, the math here threatens to be positively mind-numbing. This chapter contains a worksheet, line-by-line instructions, and illustrations to help you compute your monthly savings for retirement. However, if you're at all inclined to pursue professional financial planning assistance, this is a good place to do it. The stakes are so high when it comes to retirement planning, and the consequences of an error so dire, that in most instances it truly is "penny-wise-pound-foolish" to attempt to go it alone.

Nevertheless, the monthly retirement savings worksheet is a good starting point. Moreover, if you're in your 20s or early 30s, you may decide it's good enough—for now. Like the worksheet in the last chapter, however, there are a few cautions you should bear in mind before proceeding: (1) even a minor change in any of the variables that go into the worksheet can

FIGURE 5-1
MONTHLY SAVINGS WORKSHEET FOR RETIREMENT

1. Net Annual Retirement Income Needs

   A. Annual Retirement Income Desired (in Today's Dollars) $ _____

   B. Anticipated Annual Social Security Benefits $ _____

   C. Total Net Annual Retirement Income Needs
   (Line 1A – Line 1B) $ _____

2. Net Annual Retirement Income Needs
(in Future Dollars [from Line 1B and Figure 5-2]) $ _____

3. Total Amount Needed to Fund Net Annual Retirement
Income Needs (from Line 2 and Figure 5-3) $ _____

4. Additional Amount Needed to Fund Net Annual
Retirement Income Needs

   A. Future Value of Existing Retirement Savings
   (from Figure 5-4) $ _____

   B. Future Value of Employer's Pension (from Figure 5-6) $ _____

   C. Total Other Sources of Retirement Income Funding
   (Line 4A + Line 4B) $ _____

   D. Additional Amount Needed to Fund Net Annual
   Retirement Income Needs (Line 3 – Line 4C) $ _____

5. Total Monthly Savings Requirement

   A. Monthly Savings Amount per Thousand (from Figure 5-7) $ _____

   B. Thousands Needed (from Line 4D) $ _____

   C. Total Monthly Savings Required (Line 5A × Line 5B) $ _____

6. Additional Monthly Savings Requirement

   A. Current Monthly Savings for Retirement $ _____

   B. Additional Monthly Savings Required (Line 5C – Line 6A) $ _____

have a profound impact on the end result, especially for the long time frames associated with retirement planning; (2) a single 3.5-percent long-term inflation rate is used throughout; (3) the tables in the line-by-line instructions following the worksheet use the same conservative rounding rules discussed in the last chapter; and, (4) be sure to review the illustrations that follow the instructions—they make it much easier to see the worksheet in action.

A final caution before digging in: in working with the tables in the line-by-line instructions below, you're likely to have difficulty finding the exact numbers you need. You'll have to make informed judgments about how to read between the lines, extrapolate, and estimate in order to apply the information in the tables to your worksheet.

Line 1A. Enter the amount you anticipate you'll need to live in retirement each year on Line 1A. Because it's difficult to predict expenses in the future, it's best to think about what this will cost in today's dollars. Later in the worksheet, you'll "grow" your needs into future dollars to account for inflation.

It can be a challenge trying to predict living expenses if retirement is far off. If you're more than ten years from retirement, you may want to use a rule of thumb: you will need between 60 percent and 80 percent of your pre-retirement income in retirement. While some expenses decrease in retirement—clothing, commuting, housing (if the mortgage is paid off), others increase—health care, travel. If you plan an active retirement lifestyle, you should tend toward the high end of the range. If you look forward to a paid-off mortgage, a little gardening, and a big stack of books to read, it may be safe to stay near the low end.

If you are within ten years of your anticipated retirement, or if you are a stickler for detail, you might want to take the time to crank out a retirement budget. You can use the budget worksheet in chapter 3.

Line 1B. Popular rhetoric to the contrary notwithstanding, it is reasonable to assume that Social Security will play some role in funding your retirement income needs. Identifying that role and evaluating its reliability, however, can be problematic.

You can obtain an estimate of your annual Social Security retirement benefits from the Social Security Administration (SSA). You will need to file a Form SSA-7004-SM with the SSA in order to receive this estimate. You can obtain information about the form by visiting the SSA internet web site at http://www.ssa.gov or by calling 1-800-772-1213. The SSA Web site contains other useful information, including software you can download to estimate your Social Security retirement benefits yourself. Eventually, SSA even hopes to put individual benefits information up on its web site, but currently is beset by security concerns.

Once you make your request for benefits information, SSA will mail you a Personal Earnings and Benefits Statement—known as a PEBES. The PEBES contains a wealth of important information: the government's records of your earning history (used to compute your benefits); estimated individual retirement and disability benefits; and standard information on other Social Security benefits and how to claim them. Read your PEBES carefully, and double-check to make sure SSA has accurate records regarding your earnings history. Contact them if you note any discrepancies.

The retirement benefits estimate you obtain from your PEBES (or perhaps directly from the SSA Web site) is the starting point for the information you'll need to enter on Line 1B. You may be content to use that information as is. However, if coverage in the popular press is any barometer, most people are not comfortable relying on current benefit estimates uncritically. Many are unsure whether their estimated Social Security retirement benefits will really be there come retirement.

The outcome to this dilemma is critical to the validity of your retirement planning. However, it's hard to separate the facts from the rhetoric and figure out what to do. At the end of the day, however, two things seem certain:

1. The nation's demographics will not support the current benefits structure indefinitely, suggesting changes in benefits will have to occur at some point in the future; and,

2. The nation's leaders are unlikely to accept the political fallout that would accompany a radical departure from the current system.

What are the implications of these facts for your retirement benefits estimate? If you are within ten years of retiring, there probably aren't any. You are likely to receive the full amount of your estimate. If your personal outlook suggests otherwise, you might consider reducing the government's estimate by 10 percent, and include 90 percent of your PEBES amount on Line 1B.

If you are more than ten years from retirement, it's likely that future changes in the system will have an impact on your current PEBES estimate. It's not possible to know now the nature of that impact—a later starting date, a lower benefit amount, or some other restriction. Thus, in order to plan for a secure retirement, your assumptions need to be conservative. You should reduce the benefits estimate SSA provides by somewhere between 10 percent and 25 percent, depending on your age and outlook. Most experts say that 25 percent represents the worst-case scenario for reducing retirement benefits in order to restore actuarial balance to the Social Security Trust Fund. Enter between 75 percent and 90 percent of your current PEBES estimate on Line 1B.

You *must* obtain your PEBES in order to complete this worksheet accurately. However, if you would like to compute a "first cut" while you're waiting for the government to respond to your request for information, there are average figures you can use. SSA reports that, for an individual retiring in 1997 (the most current information available), the average annual wage is about $25,000, and the corresponding annual retirement benefit is about $11,200. The maximum benefit for someone retiring in 1997 (i.e., with wages in excess of $65,400) is just under $16,000.

If you are not covered by Social Security (or Railroad Retirement) or if you would prefer to plan for retirement without anticipating Social Security benefits, enter "0" on Line 1B.

Line 1C. Subtract Line 1B from Line 1A to compute the annual retirement income you will have to fund from resources other than Social Security—that is, from your own savings and from an employer's pension (if you have one).

Line 2. Once you know the amount of your net annual retirement income needs in today's dollars, you'll need to grow this amount for inflation. Find the amount from Line 1C in the table below, and enter the corresponding future value for it on Line 2.

FIGURE 5-2
INFLATING YOUR RETIREMENT INCOME NEEDS

Annual Income Needed In Today's Dollars	Years Until Retirement					
	5	10	15	20	30	40
10,000	12,000	14,000	17,000	20,000	28,000	40,000
15,000	18,000	21,000	25,000	30,000	42,000	60,000
20,000	24,000	28,000	34,000	40,000	56,000	80,000
25,000	30,000	35,000	42,000	50,000	70,000	99,000
30,000	36,000	42,000	50,000	60,000	84,000	119,000
40,000	48,000	56,000	67,000	80,000	112,000	158,000
50,000	60,000	70,000	84,000	100,000	140,000	198,000
75,000	89,000	106,000	126,000	150,000	210,000	297,000
100,000	120,000	141,000	168,000	200,000	281,000	396,000

Line 3. Now that you know how much money you will need for the *first* year of your retirement, you have to translate that into an amount that will fund your income needs *throughout* retirement. The table in Figure 5-3 allows you to do so. Enter on Line 3 the amount from the table that corresponds to your future annual income needs (from Line 2) and the number of years you expect to live in retirement.

Although contemplating one's mortality is never a pleasant prospect, you should be conservative in estimating how long you will live in retirement. Although dying too soon would be the worst thing that could happen to your retirement planning, running out of money would have to be a close second! Planning for a long retirement will avoid both these unfortunate problems.

FIGURE 5-3
TOTAL AMOUNT NEEDED AT RETIREMENT

Future Annual Income Needs	Anticipated Years in Retirement					
	15	20	25	30	35	40
10,000	125,000	160,000	185,000	210,000	235,000	255,000
15,000	190,000	235,000	280,000	320,000	350,000	380,000
20,000	250,000	315,000	370,000	425,000	470,000	510,000
25,000	310,000	395,000	465,000	530,000	585,000	640,000
30,000	375,000	470,000	560,000	635,000	705,000	765,000
40,000	500,000	630,000	745,000	845,000	940,000	1,020,000
50,000	625,000	785,000	930,000	1,060,000	1,175,000	1,275,000
60,000	750,000	945,000	1,115,000	1,270,000	1,405,000	1,530,000
70,000	872,000	1,100,000	1,300,000	1,480,000	1,640,000	1,785,000
80,000	995,000	1,255,000	1,490,000	1,695,000	1,875,000	2,035,000
90,000	1,120,000	1,415,000	1,675,000	1,905,000	2,110,000	2,290,000
100,000	1,245,000	1,570,000	1,860,000	2,115,000	2,345,000	2,545,000
110,000	1,370,000	1,730,000	2,045,000	2,330,000	2,580,000	2,800,000
120,000	1,495,000	1,885,000	2,235,000	2,540,000	2,815,000	3,055,000
130,000	1,620,000	2,045,000	2,420,000	2,750,000	3,050,000	3,310,000
140,000	1,745,000	2,200,000	2,605,000	2,965,000	3,280,000	3,565,000
150,000	1,870,000	2,355,000	2,790,000	3,175,000	3,515,000	3,820,000
175,000	2,180,000	2,750,000	3,255,000	3,705,000	4,105,000	4,455,000
200,000	2,490,000	3,145,000	3,720,000	4,235,000	4,690,000	5,095,000
225,000	2,805,000	3,535,000	4,185,000	4,765,000	5,275,000	5,730,000
250,000	3,115,000	3,930,000	4,650,000	5,290,000	5,860,000	6,365,000
275,000	3,425,000	4,320,000	5,110,000	5,820,000	6,445,000	7,005,000
300,000	3,740,000	4,715,000	5,580,000	6,350,000	7,035,000	7,640,000
350,000	4,360,000	5,500,000	6,510,000	7,410,000	8,205,000	8,910,000
400,000	4,985,000	6,285,000	7,440,000	8,465,000	9,380,000	10,185,000

One important thing to note about this table: in addition to the assumptions common to all of the tables (inflation and so on), it also assumes a uniform 6 percent rate of return on your "nest egg" during retirement. That is, the money you've saved for retirement will continue to earn income during your retirement, and you once again need to assume a rate of return on that savings. While 6 percent is a responsible assumption, if the actual performance of your investments in retirement varies significantly from this figure, so will the accuracy of your projections. Strategies for investment planning in retirement are discussed as part of asset allocation in chapter 7.

Line 4A. If you've already begun saving for retirement (which, of course, you have, right?) you should factor your current retirement savings into your computations. This includes both pre-tax savings (401(k)s, IRAs) and post-tax savings. As long as you are confident the amounts are earmarked for retirement, and won't be diverted to other purposes, include them here.

Some painful math is required to arrive at a figure for this part of the worksheet, so if you don't have any current retirement savings, move onto Line 4B. If you do have current retirement savings, use the worksheet below to figure out how much that savings will be worth when you retire.

FIGURE 5-4
WORKSHEET FOR GROWING RETIREMENT SAVINGS

4A-1. Total of All Current Retirement Savings	$ _____
4A-2. Future Value per Dollar (from Figure 5-5)	$ _____
4A-3. Future Value of Existing Retirement Savings (Line 1 × Line 2)	$ _____

Line 4A-1: Total all of your current retirement savings from all sources.

Line 4A-2: Find the future value of $1 from the table in Figure 5-5 that corresponds to the investment return you expect on your retirement savings and the number of years until you expect to retire. If you are unsure of how to assume an appropriate rate of return, refer to Figure 5-8 and the instructions that accompany it for more information.

Line 4A-3: Multiply Line 1 by Line 2 to obtain the total future value of your retirement savings; enter the result on Line 4A of the main worksheet.

FIGURE 5-5
FUTURE VALUE OF $1 IN SAVINGS

Assumed Rate of Return	Years to Retirement					
	5	**10**	**15**	**20**	**30**	**40**
4%	1.217	1.480	1.801	2.191	3.243	4.801
5%	1.276	1.629	2.079	2.653	4.322	7.040
6%	1.338	1.791	2.397	3.207	5.744	10.286
7%	1.403	1.967	2.759	3.870	7.612	14.975
8%	1.469	2.159	3.172	4.661	10.063	21.725
9%	1.539	2.367	3.643	5.604	13.268	31.409
10%	1.611	2.594	4.177	6.728	17.449	45.259
11%	1.685	2.839	4.785	8.062	22.892	65.001
12%	1.762	3.106	5.474	9.646	29.960	93.051

Line 4B. As with in-place retirement savings, you need to factor into your number-crunching the value of any pension you expect to receive from your employer. For purposes of this line, "pension" means only the traditional, defined-benefit employer pension historically offered by large employers—the type where the employer promises to pay you *x percent* of your salary each month in retirement. This line is not intended to cover any other type of pension plan; balances in defined contribution plans, profit sharing plans, 401(k)s, 403(b)s, 457 plans, SEPs, SIMPLEs, et cetera, all should be treated on Line 4A.

If you are covered by an employer's pension plan, you will need to assign a lump-sum value to that plan as of your retirement date. To accomplish this, you first must consult the information statement about the plan your employer is required to give you each year. That information statement tells you what your monthly (or yearly) pension benefit will be. Find the future value of that annual benefit on the table in Figure 5-6 below and enter it on Line 4B.

FIGURE 5-6

LUMP-SUM VALUE OF FIXED ANNUAL PAYMENTS

Annual Payment (in Dollars)	Years in Retirement				
	10	**15**	**20**	**30**	**40**
3,000	26,000	37,000	47,000	63,000	76,000
6,000	53,000	75,000	95,000	126,000	153,000
9,000	79,000	112,000	142,000	189,000	229,000
12,000	106,000	150,000	189,000	252,000	306,000
15,000	132,000	187,000	236,000	315,000	382,000
18,000	159,000	225,000	283,000	378,000	459,000
21,000	185,000	262,000	331,000	441,000	535,000
24,000	211,000	299,000	378,000	504,000	611,000
27,000	238,000	337,000	425,000	567,000	688,000
30,000	264,000	374,000	472,000	630,000	764,000
36,000	317,000	449,000	567,000	756,000	917,000
42,000	370,000	524,000	661,000	882,000	1,070,000
48,000	423,000	599,000	755,000	1,008,000	1,223,000
54,000	475,000	673,000	850,000	1,134,000	1,375,000
60,000	528,000	748,000	944,000	1,260,000	1,528,000
72,000	634,000	898,000	1,133,000	1,512,000	1,834,000
84,000	739,000	1,047,000	1,322,000	1,764,000	2,139,000
96,000	845,000	1,197,000	1,511,000	2,016,000	2,445,000
108,000	951,000	1,347,000	1,699,000	2,268,000	2,751,000
120,000	1,056,000	1,496,000	1,888,000	2,520,000	3,056,000

If you are saving for retirement through the purchase of an annuity, you can use Line 4B to factor that annuity into your retirement planning. Obtain the future lump-sum value of the annuity from your financial institution (or use the estimated annual annuity payment to derive a lump-sum value from Figure 5-6) and include it on Line 4B.

If you are not covered by a traditional employer's pension plan, or are not yet vested in your employer's plan, enter "0" on Line 4B.

Line 4C. Add together the amounts you entered on Lines 4A and 4B to obtain the total amount of "other sources" of retirement income.

Line 4D. Subtract Line 4C from Line 3 to determine the total additional savings you will need to have in place at retirement in order to fund your income needs throughout retirement.

Line 5A. Once you've determined the total amount you'll need at retirement, you must compute how much to save each month in order to get there. This computation requires several steps. On Line 5A, enter the amount from the table below that corresponds to the number of years until you retire and the investment return your savings will earn along the way.

FIGURE 5-7
MONTHLY SAVINGS REQUIRED PER $1,000

Assumed Rate of Return	Years to Retirement					
	5	10	15	20	30	40
4%	15.10	6.80	4.10	2.80	1.50	0.90
5%	14.70	6.50	3.80	2.50	1.20	0.70
6%	14.40	6.10	3.50	2.20	1.00	0.50
7%	14.00	5.80	3.20	2.00	0.80	0.40
8%	13.60	5.50	2.90	1.70	0.70	0.30
9%	13.30	5.20	2.70	1.50	0.60	0.20
10%	13.00	4.90	2.50	1.40	0.50	0.20
11%	12.60	4.60	2.20	1.20	0.40	0.15
12%	12.30	4.40	2.00	1.00	0.30	0.10

Note that in order to use the table above, you must assume a rate of investment return for your monthly savings. The money you save each month will be invested until you reach retirement. Regardless of where you invest your monthly savings, you will have to make an assumption about the rate of return that it will earn. Your assumption will be a product of two factors: your risk tolerance and your time frame.

Chapter 6 of this book is devoted to understanding risk and risk tolerance, as well as the relation of the two to an investment's rate of return. It even includes a short quiz to help you assess your risk tolerance. It might be helpful to review that material before attempting this part of the worksheet. However, if you want to complete a rough assessment of your monthly savings needs quickly, and are willing to accept a rule of thumb, the table below can help. Locate your risk tolerance and time frame on the table, and use the corresponding rate of return in working with Figure 5-7 above.

FIGURE 5-8
RATE OF RETURN ASSUMPTIONS—A ROUGH GUIDE

Your Risk Tolerance	Your Time Frame		
	Short (5 Years)	Medium (10 Years)	Long (10+ Years)
Low	4%	6%	8%
Average	6%	8%	10%
High	8%	10%	12%

Line 5B. The information you computed for Line 5A only tells you how much you need to save for $1,000. Now you have to multiply that amount by the number of thousands in your goal. For example, if Line 4D indicates you need to save an additional $500,000, you would enter 500 on Line 5B; for $750,000, you would enter 750 on Line 5B; and so on.

Line 5C. To compute your total monthly savings requirement, multiply the monthly savings amount per thousand (Line 5A) by the number of thousands needed to reach your goal (Line 5B).

Line 6A. If you're already setting aside an amount each month for retirement, for example in a 401(k) or through monthly investments in a mutual fund, and you plan to continue setting this amount aside each month, enter it on Line 6A.

Line 6B. Subtract the amount on Line 6A from the amount on Line 5C to determine the additional amount you'll have to save each month in order to achieve your retirement planning goal.

ILLUSTRATION

> Tran is 35 years old and earns $60,000. He wants to retire at age 65 and anticipates a very active retirement lifestyle. While his house will be paid off by then, he knows he will have high property taxes and maintenance fees. Because of his planned retirement lifestyle, Tran estimates that his retirement income needs will be 75 percent of his current income (i.e., $45,000). Tran has received a statement from the Social Security Administration indicating that his monthly retirement benefits will be about $1,000, or $12,000 annually. Tran expects to live a full thirty years in retirement. He has not yet begun saving for retirement. Tran describes his risk tolerance as average, and he expects his investments to earn a 10 percent rate of return.

FIGURE 5-9
TRAN'S MONTHLY SAVINGS WORKSHEET FOR RETIREMENT

1. Net Annual Retirement Income Needs:

    A. Annual Retirement Income Desired (in Today's Dollars) $45,000

    B. Anticipated Annual Social Security Benefits $12,000

    C. Total Net Annual Retirement Income Needs
    (Line 1A – Line 1B) $33,000

2. Net Annual Retirement Income Needs
    (in Future Dollars [from Line 1B and Figure 5-2]) $90,000

3. Total Amount Needed to Fund Net Annual
    Retirement Income Needs (from Line 2 and Figure 5-3) $1,900,000

4. Additional Amount Needed to Fund Net Annual Retirement Income Needs:

    A. Future Value of Existing Retirement Savings
    (from Figure 5-4)   0

    B. Future Value of Employer's Pension (from Figure 5-6)   0

continues

(continued)
TRAN'S MONTHLY SAVINGS WORKSHEET FOR RETIREMENT

C. Total Other Sources of Retirement Income Funding (Line 4A + Line 4B)	0
D. Additional Amount Needed to Fund Net Annual Retirement Income Needs (Line 3 – Line 4C)	$1,900,000
5. Total Monthly Savings Requirement	
A. Monthly Savings Amount per Thousand (from Figure 5-7)	$0.50
B. Thousands Needed (from Line 4D)	1900
C. Total Monthly Savings Required (Line 5A × Line 5B)	$950
6. Additional Monthly Savings Requirement	
A. Current Monthly Savings for Retirement	$0
B. Additional Monthly Savings Required (Line 5C – Line 6A)	$950

ILLUSTRATION

Same facts as above, but assume that Tran contributes $250 per month to a 401(k) plan, and his vested balance in the plan is $25,000.

FIGURE 5-10
TRAN'S REVISED MONTHLY SAVINGS WORKSHEET FOR RETIREMENT

1. Net Annual Retirement Income Needs:	
A. Annual Retirement Income Desired (in Today's Dollars)	$45,000
B. Anticipated Annual Social Security Benefits	$12,000
C. Total Net Annual Retirement Income Needs (Line 1A – Line 1B)	$33,000
2. Net Annual Retirement Income Needs (in Future Dollars [from Line 1B and Figure 5-2])	$90,000
3. Total Amount Needed to Fund Net Annual Retirement Income Needs (from Line 2 and Figure 5-3)	$1,900,000

continues

(continued)

TRAN'S REVISED MONTHLY
SAVINGS WORKSHEET FOR RETIREMENT

4. Additional Amount Needed to Fund Net Annual Retirement Income Needs:

A. Future Value of Existing Retirement Savings (from Figure 5-4)	$436,225
B. Future Value of Employer's Pension (from Figure 5-6)	$0
C. Total Other Sources of Retirement Income Funding (Line 4A + Line 4B)	$436,225
D. Additional Amount Needed to Fund Net Annual Retirement Income Needs (Line 3 – Line 4C)	$1,463,775

5. Total Monthly Savings Requirement

A. Monthly Savings Amount per Thousand (from Figure 5-7)	$0.50
B. Thousands Needed (from Line 4D)	1,464
C. Total Monthly Savings Required (Line 5A × Line 5B)	$732

6. Additional Monthly Savings Requirement

A. Current Monthly Savings for Retirement	$250
B. Additional Monthly Savings Required (Line 5C – Line 6A)	$482

Note that in the last illustration, Tran needed to complete the following worksheet in order to enter an amount on Line 4A.

FIGURE 5-11
WORKSHEET FOR GROWING
TRAN'S CURRENT RETIREMENT SAVINGS

4A-1. Total of All Current Retirement Savings	$25,000
4A-2. Future Value per Dollar (from Figure 5-5)	17.449
4A-3. Future Value of Existing Retirement Savings (Line 1 × Line 2)	$436,225

The contrast between these two illustrations highlights several important points. First, you should start saving for retirement early; by already having $25,000 in a 401(k) in the second illustration, Tran knocked more than a third off what he needed to save each month for retirement. Time is your biggest ally in saving for retirement. Next, employer's retirement plans matter—take advantage of them. Contribute the maximum possible to all retirement plans. Finally, the worksheet is imperfect; note that Tran had to extrapolate from Figure 5-2 to arrive at the $90,000 amount entered on Line 2. This reinforces the need for accurate professional assistance to supplement the work you've done here.

As in the last chapter, the results from the worksheet here do not take into account any tax due on the earnings from your investments. In order to achieve your goal, those taxes will need to be paid from other sources. Especially in the case of retirement, there are investment vehicles that can help you save on a tax-deferred basis. Again, refer to chapter 17 for these and other ways to minimize taxes and maximize savings.

What If It Doesn't Work?

What happens if you've gone through the worksheet, and you can't achieve your retirement goal within your time frame given your risk tolerance? As in the last chapter, the answer is that one of the variables must be changed. You either have to adjust the amount of your goal, lengthen your time frame, or increase your risk tolerance in order to earn a higher rate of return.

ILLUSTRATION

You are 45 years old. Your goal is to retire at age 60 with $40,000 per year in retirement income. After taking into account Social Security and your employer's pension, you determine you will need to save an additional $100,000 by age 60 to meet your goal. You can afford to invest $250 per month toward this goal. However, you project that the only investments suitable to your risk tolerance and time frame will produce $85,000, leaving you $15,000 short. The $85,000 figure would allow for retirement income of only $38,000 per year. (If you worked through the last chapter, the numbers in this illustration should sound familiar!)

Option 1. You decide to alter your annual retirement income goal from $40,000 to $38,000, and save, invest, and retire as planned.

Option 2. You decide that you will need the full $40,000 per year in retirement. You increase your monthly investment from $250 to $300 by reallocating $50 from your monthly entertainment/vacation expenditures to reach your goal.

Option 3. You alter your time frame and continue working until age 62 to reach your $100,000 retirement savings goal.

Option 4. You conclude that if you accept slightly more risk, you can find investments that will enable you to meet your $100,000 retirement savings goal by age 60 by investing only $250 per month.

As the last chapter emphasized, it is difficult for a person to alter his or her risk tolerance. If a major departure in your current risk tolerance would be required to reach your goal, Option 4 probably isn't appropriate for you.

Retirement Planning for Lesbian and Gay Couples

The worksheet in this chapter contemplates retirement planning for a single person. Lesbian and gay couples generally should plan for retirement individually. There are several reasons for this. First, Social Security will not pay spousal or survivor benefits to gay couples. Second, if one partner were to die before retirement, any amount from an employer's pension (i.e., amounts contemplated on Line 4B) would not be available to his or her surviving partner. Finally, it is necessary to allow for the possibility that the relationship will have ended by the time one or the other partner reaches retirement. Without the protections for retirement savings that come from legal divorce, there is no way to ensure equitable distribution of joint retirement assets.

For couples who plan individually, each partner should be sure to make appropriate adjustments to the initial estimate of retirement income needs on Line 1A to ensure that living expenses are not double-counted.

PART III

Building a Portfolio: Investment Planning

CHAPTER 6

Understanding Risk

Almost everybody is an investor, whether they think of themselves in such terms or not. If you have any assets or any income, you make investment decisions about them. Again, you may not think of your actions as investment decisions, but they are.

ILLUSTRATION

Philippe has arranged for direct deposit of his weekly pay into his checking account. He uses his checking account to pay rent, utilities, his car loan, and other monthly expenses. If he has any money left at the end of the month, he leaves it in his checking account to help with the next month's expenses. By taking these actions, Philippe has made choices regarding his financial planning *goal* (an emergency fund), his *time frame* (short), his *risk tolerance* (low), the *rate of return* he expects on his investments (low), his *asset allocation* (a checking account), and his *individual investment selection* (the particular bank he uses).

The italicized terms in this illustration represent the building blocks of solid investment planning. Some of them should sound familiar to you: goals and time frames were discussed in chapter 1. The purpose of this chapter and the three that follow it is to provide you with a deeper understanding of the other terms: risk tolerance, rate of return, asset allocation, and individual investment selection. By helping you determine what to do with your monthly savings, investment planning allows you to turn a financial planning goal into reality.

RISK AND SOURCES OF INVESTMENT RISK

In its broadest sense, investment risk refers to the possibility that an investment's performance will deviate from expectations, with the result that you will be unable to achieve your financial goal.

Financial planners often speak of nine sources of potential investment risk. It's important to understand that *every* investment carries one or more forms of risk, and that there is no such thing as a risk-free investment. Once you review these sources of risk, you'll see that even a government-insured bank account or money under the mattress carries some form of risk.

1. **Market Risk.** The risk that the value of a particular investment will decrease as a result of overall decreases in the market in which the investment is traded. Stocks, stock mutual funds, stock futures, stock options, and real estate are subject to market risk.

2. **Interest Rate Risk.** The risk that changes in interest rates will lower the value of an investment. If you own a bond paying 8 percent, and the prevailing interest rate is 9 percent at the time you decide to sell your bond, you will have to discount your sales price in order to induce a potential buyer to accept the lower interest rate your bond carries. Bonds and bond mutual funds are subject to interest rate risk.

3. **Reinvestment Risk.** The risk that you will be unable to reinvest the proceeds of an investment (interest, dividends, or returned principal) at the same rate of return as the original investment due to changes in market conditions. Stocks, stock mutual funds, bonds, bond mutual funds, and certificates of deposit are subject to reinvestment risk.

4. **Inflation Risk.** The risk that the return on your investment will not be sufficient to keep pace with inflation. Because of their low rates of return, all cash and cash equivalent investments (savings accounts, money markets, and certificates of deposit) are subject to inflation risk.

5. **Exchange Rate Risk.** The risk that the return on foreign investments will be reduced as a result of changes in the value of the currency in which the investment is traded relative to the U.S. dollar. With this form of risk, the value of the underlying investment may remain unchanged, but because of fluctuations in foreign currency exchange rates, you may lose money when you convert your investment back into U.S. dollars. Foreign stocks, foreign bonds, foreign mutual funds, international mutual funds, and foreign real estate are subject to exchange rate risk.

6. **Liquidity Risk.** The risk that an investment cannot be quickly sold ("liquidated") at its full value due to an inability to find interested buyers. Stocks and bonds issued by small companies and real estate are subject to liquidity risk.

7. **Business Risk.** The risk associated with investing in a particular firm or industry. Business risk can result from government regulation, the availability of skilled workers, new technologies that make old products obsolete, or even the competence of a firm's management. Individual stocks, individual bonds, and sector mutual funds are subject to business risk.

8. **Financial Risk.** The risk that comes from using too much debt to finance a business' operations. Individual stocks, individual bonds, and certain investment real estate are subject to financial risk.

9. **Default Risk.** The risk that an investment may stop making required payments dues to financial hardship, insolvency, or even bankruptcy. Bonds (other than bonds issued by the U.S. government) are subject to default risk.

Relationship Between Risk and Return

It's important to understand the sources of investment risk in order to appreciate the relationship between risk and an investment's rate of return. In a nutshell, the higher an investment's overall risk, the greater its return should be. The theory behind this is that you should receive a greater return if you are willing to assume more risk with your money.

Over time, investment professionals have come to understand the risks associated with various types of investments, and the relative return each type earns tends to reflect that understanding. Traditionally, this relationship is expressed in the form of a pyramid. The various types of investments are listed in ascending order on the pyramid; the higher up the pyramid you go, the greater the risk—and the return. A sample "risk pyramid" is contained in Figure 6-1.

HIGH

Small Capitalization Stock Funds
Sector Mutual Funds
Value Mutual Funds
International Mutual Funds
Real Estate Investment Trusts
Growth Mutual Funds
Growth & Income Mutual Funds
High Grade Corporate Bond Mutual Funds
High Grade Municipal Bond Mutual Funds
U.S. Government Securities
Certificates of Deposit
Money Markets
Checking & Savings Accounts

RISK   RETURN

LOW

FIGURE 6-1
RISK PYRAMID

Don't worry for now if the names of some of the investment types in the risk pyramid sound unfamiliar; they all will be explained in the next chapter.

Measuring Your Risk Tolerance

Your ability to accept actual short-term decreases in the value of your portfolio is known as your *risk tolerance*. There are many ways to measure risk tolerance; you probably have an intuitive sense of your own already. Although there are sophisticated techniques for distinguishing subtle nuances between various levels of risk tolerance, for now you'll want to stick to three familiar measurements: low, average, and high. The figure below contains a simple "test" that will help you determine which of these three labels best describes your risk tolerance.

FIGURE 6-2
RISK TOLERANCE TEST

1. Choose one:

   a. A sure gain of $2,500

   b. A 25% chance of a $10,000 gain and a 75% chance of 0 gain

2. Due to a general market correction, one of your investments loses 15% of its value three months after you purchase it. Do you:

   a. Sell the investment to avoid any further losses?

   b. Hold the investment and wait to see what happens?

   c. Buy more now that the price is down?

3. Your friend has started a new business. He asks you to invest. The failure rate for small businesses in your friend's field is 80%. However, if the business succeeds, you will earn 50% on your investment in 12 months. Do you invest:

   a. Nothing

   b. One month's salary

   c. Three month's salary

4. Which statement best describes you:

   a. I can tolerate infrequent, very moderate losses through difficult phases in an overall market cycle

   b. I can tolerate two or three quarters of negative returns through difficult phases in the overall market cycle

   c. I can tolerate more than one year of negative returns through difficult phases in the overall market cycle

5. What is the maximum loss you will tolerate in any one year?

   a. –2%

   b. –5%

   c. –10%

Give yourself one point for every "a" answer, two points for every "b", and three points for every "c." Add up all your points and find your risk tolerance below:

continues

(continued)

Total Points	Risk Tolerance
5–7	Low
8–11	Average
12–14	High

You'll use this understanding of your risk tolerance for projecting monthly savings needs (in chapters 4 and 5) and for selecting an appropriate asset allocation strategy for your portfolio (in the next chapter).

DIVERSIFICATION

Now that you know about the various sources of investment risk, the risk levels associated with various types of investments, and your own risk tolerance, it's time to think about ways to handle risk. Because investment risk *cannot* be eliminated, you must use strategies that will minimize it. The single best strategy for minimizing risk is *diversification*.

Investment theorists and the professional planners who read their works spend years studying the most efficient ways to diversify a portfolio. Here's what you can learn from their efforts: diversifying your portfolio among a number of properly-selected individual investments will lower your risk.

ILLUSTRATION

Kishma has $1,000 to invest. If she invests it all in stock X, the entire $1,000 is subject to the business risk of that company. If she invests $500 in stock X and $500 in stock Y, she has lowered her risk through (modest) diversification. If stocks X and Y are in different industries (for example, technology and health care), she has lowered her risk even more.

ILLUSTRATION

In the last illustration, if Kishma instead invested her $1,000 in a mutual fund, she could spread her risk literally among hundreds of companies and dozens of industries, achieving a level of diversification not possible through direct investment in individual stocks and bonds.

This latter illustration raises an important point: it's much easier for average investors to achieve diversification through mutual funds than through "direct" investments in individual securities (stocks and bonds).

You may have noticed that the risk pyramid above didn't list individual securities, just mutual funds. That's because it's hard to assess the unique mix of risks present in any individual issue. In other words, any single stock or bond could fall almost anywhere on the pyramid, making generalizations impossible. This has implications for your ability to diversify: if diversification is about spreading risk around in order to lower it, that can be hard to do when investing in individual securities. If the risk from any individual security could fall anywhere on the pyramid, then it's likely to require a great number of individual securities to produce a low average risk (i.e., a properly diversified portfolio). Moreover, the less money you have to invest, the fewer individual securities you will be able to purchase, making an acceptable average even harder to achieve.

It's tempting to want to invest in individual securities, to feel like a "player" with your investments. However, unless your investment portfolio is large enough that you can achieve comparable diversification through direct investments—and this probably means in excess of $100,000—you generally are better off sticking to mutual funds.

Are there any rules of thumb to help you know the number of individual investments that should be in your portfolio? After all, even if you invest through mutual funds, you'll need to diversify your portfolio among several different ones. While the answer to this question will vary somewhat depending on the size of your portfolio (more money means more investment choices), you generally should diversify among at least four and up to twelve mutual funds, or at least twelve and up to thirty individual securities. The logic behind this rule of thumb is pretty simple: go any lower, and you risk being inadequately diversified; go any higher, and you probably won't be able to adequately monitor your investments' ongoing performance.

CHAPTER 7

Asset Allocation Strategies

I n chapters 4 and 5, you calculated how much to save each month in order to reach a specific financial planning goal. As part of your calculations, you made some assumptions about what would happen to your savings along the way. In this part of the book, you will learn how to use asset allocation to ensure that your investment assumptions enable you to achieve your goals.

Asset allocation refers to the process of dividing your portfolio into three broad categories: cash equivalent investments, income investments, and growth investments. The purpose of these categories is to provide structure and discipline to the process of selecting investments; in other words, to help ensure that the investments in your portfolio are suitable for achieving your goal within your time frame and given your risk tolerance.

You should have noticed the reference to "*your* portfolio" in the first paragraph, as well as throughout the last chapter. Whether you've ever thought of it as such, you do have a portfolio. It consists of all the assets listed in the cash equivalents and invested assets sections of your balance sheet. The strategies discussed in this chapter can help you determine whether or not the way you've divided your money among the various investments listed on your balance sheet—in other words your asset allocation—is right for you.

In trying to understand what asset allocation is and how it works, it may be helpful to think of your portfolio as being divided into three buckets (cash equivalents, income, and growth). Depending on what you want your portfolio to accomplish (your goals and your time frame), you will need to fill each bucket with different amounts and different types of liquids.

Before learning how to fill your buckets, you need to understand the differences between the labels attached to each. *Cash equivalent investments* can be liquidated quickly with no risk of short-term fluctuation in value due to market conditions; examples include savings accounts, money market accounts, certificates of deposit, and 90-day U.S. Treasury bills. *Income investments* are intended to provide a steady source of current income with nominal risk of short-term fluctuation in value due to market conditions; examples include bonds, bond mutual funds, and some high-dividend stocks. *Growth investments* are intended to provide long-term growth in asset value, with or without current income, and with appreciable to significant risk of short-term fluctuation in value due to market conditions; examples include stocks, stock mutual funds, and real estate.

If you reflect on the risk pyramid in the last chapter, you'll recall that higher-risk investments offer higher returns. Thus, income investments can be expected to provide higher returns than cash equivalent investments do, and growth investments higher returns than either of the other asset classes do.

Because of the different characteristics of each bucket (asset class), it's not hard to intuit that some buckets are better suited to certain goals and time frames than others. In general, the longer your time frame, the more you'll need to put in the growth bucket. Again, asset allocation is the process that helps you decide what amount of your assets to pour into each bucket.

The following set of tables offers one widely-accepted model for making asset allocations; you should use it as a guideline for determining the allocations right for you. Find the table that corresponds to your risk tolerance, which you identified in the last chapter.

FIGURE 7-1
SAMPLE ASSET ALLOCATIONS
FOR INVESTORS WITH LOW RISK TOLERANCE

Time Frame	Cash	Income	Growth
Current Income	60%	40%	0%
Short (< 5 years)	50%	30%	20%

continues

(continued)

Time Frame	Cash	Income	Growth
Medium (5–15 years)	30%	40%	30%
Long (> 15 years)	20%	40%	40%

FIGURE 7-2
SAMPLE ASSET ALLOCATIONS
FOR INVESTORS WITH AVERAGE RISK TOLERANCE

Time Frame	Cash	Income	Growth
Current Income	40%	40%	20%
Short (< 5 years)	30%	50%	20%
Medium (5–15 years)	20%	50%	30%
Long (> 15 years)	10%	30%	60%

FIGURE 7-3
SAMPLE ASSET ALLOCATIONS
FOR INVESTORS WITH HIGH RISK TOLERANCE

Time Frame	Cash	Income	Growth
Current Income	30%	50%	20%
Short (< 5 years)	30%	40%	30%
Medium (5–15 years)	10%	50%	40%
Long (> 15 years)	0%	30%	70%

Don't accept the recommendations contained in these tables uncritically. If your risk tolerance or time frames are at one end or the other of a given range, you should make adjustments to the allocation percentages above.

ILLUSTRATION

Fred's risk tolerance is very low and the time frame for his investment goal is three years. Fred does not believe he can absorb the risk involved in the allocations recommended above because of his time frame, so he adjusts his allocation from 50% cash equivalent, 30% income, and 20% growth to 60% cash equivalent, 30% income, and 10% growth.

Keep in mind that, as you get closer to reaching your goal, your time frame shortens and you may need to adjust your allocation strategy accordingly. One example of where this is sure to arise: as you get closer to retirement, your time frame will shift from long-term to medium-term to short-term, and finally to the need for current income once you reach retirement age.

Also keep in mind that time frames can be an issue even after you reach certain goals. Again using retirement as an example, your retirement savings probably will need to last twenty, thirty, or perhaps even forty years. These are the time frames normally associated with long-term investment goals. You thus will have to balance your need for current income with a need for continued long-term growth, and adopt an asset allocation model that blends the two needs. This might be accomplished by segregating a portion of your savings when you retire, assigning a medium- or long-term time frame to that portion, and investing it accordingly. Later in retirement, you can reallocate that portion to satisfy your current income needs.

ILLUSTRATION

Louise has just retired at age 65. Her health is excellent, and she thinks it is reasonable to expect she may live twenty to thirty years in retirement. She uses current income allocations for 60 percent of her retirement savings, and long-term allocations for the other 40 percent. She plans to revisit her allocations every five years.

Whenever you're trying to invest for more than one goal simultaneously, the segregation approach explained above also can help.

ILLUSTRATION

Jeannie, age 27, is saving both to buy a house by age 30 and for retirement. She currently has $40,000 to invest, and saves $350 per month. Jeannie uses long-term allocations for 70 percent of her savings (for retirement), and short-term allocations for the other 30 percent (for the house).

After you've chosen the right way to allocate your portfolio, you're ready to focus on selecting individual investments.

CHAPTER 8

Selecting Individual Investments

Most investors agonize over the selection of individual investments. To be sure, it is an important decision, but it turns out that the asset allocation work you've done in the last chapter is the most important factor influencing your portfolio's performance. According to one famous study, proper asset allocation accounts for over 90 percent of the variation in a portfolio's performance; several other factors, including individual investment selection, make up the other 8 percent +. Here's one illustration of how this can happen:

ILLUSTRATION

You are an investor with average risk tolerance and long-term goals. Because you don't understand investment planning, you allocate 80 percent of the assets in your 401(k) plan to a money market fund, and 20 percent to a growth fund. The return for the money market is 5 percent (above average for this type of investment), and the return for the growth fund is 10 percent (below average for this type of investment). Even though the money market is a star performer for its group, its return can't match the growth fund's—and growth is what all investors need for long-term goals like retirement.

This illustration isn't altogether hypothetical, either. Another recent study found that almost 80 percent of 401(k) participants have under-allocated their portfolios; that is, they have not allocated enough toward the growth investments they'll need to achieve their retirement goals. Proper asset allocation is essential to the performance of your portfolio.

Before you can complete your investment planning, however, you still must decide which investments to select from within each asset class—what to fill each bucket with, if you recall the analogy from the last chapter. There are a number of important things you'll need to know in order to make good decisions when selecting individual assets. The most important of these is to recall the diversification discussion in chapter 6. Again, in order to be properly diversified, your portfolio should include at least four and perhaps as many as twelve different mutual fund investments.

Note that this chapter assumes you are investing through mutual funds, rather than directly in individual securities. Although mutual funds are more appropriate for most investors and most investment goals, if you do have a portfolio large enough to warrant investing in individual securities, the strategies discussed below will work for you, too.

Allocating Within an Asset Class

Sometimes, you may only have a limited number of investment selections available to you. This is common in the case of most 401(k) plans, where you generally only have access to between four and eight different mutual funds. Annuities also offer only a limited number of investment options. In some respects, your job becomes a little easier in these circumstances; once you've established the right asset allocation, you need only choose which of the available options best fits within each of your asset classes. If more than one option will work for any portion of your desired portfolio allocation, you either should eliminate any weak performers or divide your assets among the acceptable options.

On the other hand, if your investment selections are not limited in this way, you may need to do a little additional allocating within each asset class before selecting individual investments. Consider the following:

1. It's usually a good idea to include some exposure to foreign assets in a growth portfolio. There are two reasons for this. First, foreign markets don't always run in the same economic cycle as U.S. markets, and investments there can provide a cushioning effect on your portfolio when the U.S. market is down. Second, in many developing nations, the long-term potential for real growth is greater than

in mature economies like the U.S. and Western Europe. Although the ride in these "emerging markets" is sure to be bumpy, the long-term results are promising. Broad diversification is essential with international investments in order for these considerations to be of any value to your portfolio.

2. If you are investing for long-term goals, and your risk tolerance is average or high, you should include some higher risk investments, like value funds or aggressive growth funds, in your growth portfolio.

3. If you are investing for medium- or long-term goals, and your portfolio is substantial, consider including some exposure to real estate through a real estate investment trust (REIT). Mortgage REITs add a nice element of diversification to large income portfolios, and equity REITs do the same for growth portfolios.

If any of these considerations have appeal to you, you might decide to allocate within an asset class in order to take advantage of the opportunities they present.

ILLUSTRATION

Bruno has average risk tolerance and is investing for long-term goals. He recognizes the value of incorporating international investments into his portfolio, and decides to allocate 15 percent of his growth portfolio to a foreign growth fund.

Beyond these special considerations, the individual investment selections you make within each asset class are largely a function of the investment alternatives and information you (and your financial planner or investment advisor) are able to identify and obtain. The balance of this chapter is devoted to helping you understand specific types of investments and to finding and using tools to make good investment selections.

TYPES OF GROWTH INVESTMENTS

The risk pyramid in chapter 6 (Figure 6-1) contains several types of growth investments you are likely to encounter as you select individual investments:

1. **Growth And Income Mutual Funds.** These funds set both long-term growth and current income as equal objectives. They typically choose investments that offer both current dividends and the potential for long-term growth.

2. **Growth Mutual Funds.** These funds invest primarily for long-term growth; they usually provide only modest current income.

3. **Real Estate Investment Trusts.** Real estate investment trusts (REITs) come in two varieties. Equity REITs invest in properties (commercial, residential, hotels, storage facilities) the management believes will produce a steady income stream and/or appreciate in value. Mortgage REITs invest in mortgages secured by real estate. By investing in multiple properties, REITs minimize some of the risks traditionally associated with investing in real estate.

4. **International Mutual Funds.** These funds invest primarily in growth investments (although there are dedicated international bond funds). Some funds invest only in foreign investments, others include U.S. investments in their portfolios. Some funds are specific to certain geographic areas (Latin America, Asia), and others target so-called emerging markets.

5. **Value Mutual Funds.** The managers of these funds try to find companies they believe have been under-valued in the market, and therefore offer the potential for above-average growth opportunities.

6. **Sector Mutual Funds.** These funds limit their investments to a single industry (e.g., technology, health care). Investors who believe a particular industry presents above-average growth opportunities use these funds as a way to obtain a diversified portfolio within that industry.

7. **Small Capitalization Stock Mutual Funds.** These funds invest in small or start-up ventures where the potential for growth is well above average. Given the failure rate of small and start-up businesses, however, these funds also present risk levels well above average.

8. **Aggressive Growth Stock Mutual Funds.** These funds take significant risk with principal to pursue above-average growth opportunities. They may seek under-valued companies or start-up companies;

they may assume higher diversification risks by concentrating in one or two industries or securities in which the fund manager believes there is above-average growth potential. The knowledge and experience of the mutual fund manager takes on extra importance with aggressive growth funds.

TYPES OF INCOME INVESTMENTS

The risk pyramid in chapter 6 (Figure 6-1) also identified several types of income investments:

1. **U.S. Government Securities.** The U.S. Treasury issues three types of securities, classified by their maturity: *Treasury bills* are short-term debt (less than fifty-two weeks); *Treasury notes* are intermediate-term debt (two to ten years); and *Treasury bonds* are long-term debt (ten to thirty years). These securities are backed by the full faith and credit of the U.S. government, making them virtually free of default risk. In order to purchase Treasuries directly, a minimum investment of $5,000 ($10,000 for bills) is required; alternatively, they can be purchased through mutual funds. Agencies of the U.S. government also issue bonds (e.g., mortgage-backed "Ginnie Maes"); although these, too, have the full faith and credit of the U.S. government, they tend to be more susceptible to interest rate risk, and therefore offer slightly higher returns.

2. **High Grade Municipal Bond Mutual Funds.** These funds invest in bonds issued by state and local governments. The bonds are used to finance either general obligations or specific projects (airports, highways, sports facilities). Occasionally, a municipality will default on its obligations, and the creditworthiness of municipal bonds is a consideration. Generally, municipal bond mutual funds don't invest in low-grade bonds, but be sure to investigate for this possibility; such investments are not appropriate for income portfolios. Usually, the income from "munis" is exempt from federal tax; these tax advantages are detailed in chapter 17.

3. **High Grade Corporate Bond Mutual Funds.** These funds invest in bonds issued by private companies. Creditworthiness is an important factor in determining a bond's value; most corporate bond

mutual funds invest only in high grade bonds. There are funds that specialize in high risk bonds (*junk bonds*), but these funds are too speculative for most investors.

EVALUATING INVESTMENT PERFORMANCE

In order to know how to select among the available investment alternatives, you need some basis for measuring performance. The business sections of major daily newspapers are one source, but usually you'll want more detail. For this, you should turn to one of the private companies that rate investment performance: Morningstar, Lipper, Value-Line, and Standard & Poors are four common sources. Their materials are available at most libraries and (in varying degrees) over the internet. They will be able to provide you with information about an investment's past performance (its historical return), investment objectives (growth or income), portfolio composition (for mutual funds), creditworthiness (for bonds), and so on.

One of the most important pieces of information you can obtain about an investment is its historical performance. Although it is more than a cliché that "past performance is no guarantee of future returns," historical data at least allow you to compare how an investment performed against comparable investments. To do this, you would compare the investment against its *benchmark*—a widely-publicized measure of the performance of broad classes of investments or markets. Investments that do not at least meet their benchmark should be avoided.

Table 8-1 provides statistics for several benchmarks you can use to evaluate the performance of investments—either those you are considering or those already in your portfolio. This information is current through June 30, 1997; you should obtain current information from one of the sources above before making any major investment decisions.

Fundamental Analysis

In a way, it's interesting that so much energy is devoted to reviewing an investment's past performance. After all, are you investing for the past or for the future? Past performance is a helpful way to comparison-shop, but it doesn't tell the complete story. In order to fully understand whether your investment selection is a good one, you must engage in what financial planners refer to as *fundamental analysis*.

FIGURE 8-1
IMPORTANT BENCHMARKS
FOR INVESTMENT PERFORMANCE

Type of Investment	Benchmark	3 Yr Return	5 Yr Return	10 Yr Return
Inflation	CPI	2.65	2.69	3.50
Treasury Bills	90-day Treasury Bill	5.17	4.38	5.44
Treasury Notes	Lehman Brothers Intermediate Treasury Index	7.14	6.04	7.84
Treasury Bonds	Lehman Brothers Long-term Treasury Bond Index	10.22	9.04	9.85
Municipal Bonds	Lehman Brothers Municipal Bond Index	7.91	7.22	8.18
Corporate Bonds	Lehman Brothers Corporate Bond Index	9.60	8.03	9.47
Growth Stocks	S&P 500	28.83	19.76	14.65
Small Cap Stocks	Russell 2000	20.07	17.88	11.14
REITs	Wilshire REIT Index	16.36	16.33	7.99
International	MSCI EAFE Stocks (Morgan Stanley)	9.12	12.83	6.58

Fundamental analysis requires taking a hard look at the economic fundamentals of an investment. More than evaluating numbers and returns, it requires you to get to know a lot about the environment in which a potential investment operates. Relevant questions include:

1. What is the current overall economic climate, and what impact is it likely to have on the investment?

2. What is the state of the industry in which the investment operates, and how might any changes impact the investment's performance?

3. For stocks, is the price supported by the company's earnings?

4. For bonds, what is the investment's creditworthiness?

5. For mutual funds, what recent changes have occurred (or may occur) among the fund's management?

This last point merits further consideration: mutual fund performance is in no small measure driven by the knowledge and experience of its managers. If there are major changes in management at a mutual fund, you may wish to defer making new or additional investments in the fund until new managers are in place and can be evaluated (assuming acceptable alternative investments exist).

Transaction Costs

It, of course, costs money to buy, sell, and hold investments—sales commissions, mutual fund loads, sales charges, custodial fees, and mutual fund 12(b)(1) fees. All these fees have an impact on an investment's return.

ILLUSTRATION

Investment X yields an annual return of 8.9 percent; Investment Y yields 9.5 percent. Y appears to be the better. However, Y also imposes various transaction fees totaling 1 percent per year; X has no such fees. X is actually a better investment.

It is possible to find mutual fund investments that do not charge sales fees; all things being equal, these "no-load" funds will save you money. For this reason, some financial planners recommend that you only invest in no-loads. However, some "load" funds give you the option of either paying a commission up front (buying so-called "A shares"), or investing without a commission as long as you agree to keep your investment for five or so years ("B shares"). B shares make more sense for a long-term investor with a buy-and-hold strategy; be warned, however, that there will be a small penalty if you sell B shares too soon. Finally, if you are considering an investment with a sales commission, be suspicious of rates in excess of 5 percent or 6 percent; they may be worth paying, but only if the return is well above the benchmark.

Mutual funds also charge annual management fees called "12(b)(1)" fees. Unlike loads, all funds charge annual fees. Fees generally average 1 percent to 2 percent; lower fees are a good sign, and higher ones can only be justified by superior performance.

You should always fully investigate loads and fees (they're disclosed on the investment prospectus), and be sure to consider them when comparing the performance of two investments.

Style Slippage

Over time, a mutual fund's actual portfolio may vary somewhat from its stated objectives. For example, an aggressive growth fund cannot invest 100 percent of its assets in aggressive growth stocks; some assets must be kept in cash in order to buy new stocks, pay shareholders who leave the fund, cover administrative fees, etc. A little of this is to be expected; however, when it goes to far, or occurs deliberately (because a fund manager invests outside the objective in order to achieve a higher return), it's known as *style slippage*. Because proper asset allocation is essential to the performance of your portfolio, severe style slippage could be a problem; periodic review of the information found in Morningstar or one of the other rating services can minimize this risk.

Reviewing Your Portfolio

Once you've made your individual investment selections and your portfolio is in place, you may be tempted to think your work is finished. Not quite— two ongoing tasks are required.

First, you must consciously adopt a buy-and-hold strategy, particularly with respect to your growth investments. You are investing for the long-haul, and you should not panic at the first sign of trouble. If you have allocated within your risk tolerance, this should not be a problem. Similarly, you should not make rash decisions based on "hot tips" or similar factors. Remember, every time you buy and sell, you run the risk of incurring additional transaction costs.

Second, you will need to periodically review your investments to ensure that they continue to remain appropriate for your goals and time frames. Moreover, you should compare the performance of your investments to their appropriate benchmarks to ensure your returns are adequate. Again, while you should not sell investments based on short-term disappointments, neither should you keep ones that demonstrate a serious and extended pattern of under-performance *vis-à-vis* their benchmark. Criteria for doing this are recommended in chapter 24.

CHAPTER 9

Other Investment Strategies

Before leaving the topic of investment planning, there are a few other strategies you should be aware of. Some of them should certainly be included in your investment planning, the utility of others will depend on your circumstances, and one you should know about simply in order to be sure you avoid it.

DIVIDEND REINVESTMENT PROGRAMS

Dividend reinvestment programs (DRIPs) allow you to reinvest the dividends you receive from an individual stock or a mutual fund, purchasing additional shares of the investment.

ILLUSTRATION

You own 100 shares of ABC fund, which currently trades for $25 per share. ABC pays quarterly dividends of 50 cents per share. If you participate in ABC's DRIP, the mutual fund simply adds two additional shares to your account when it pays dividends ($50 in dividends/$25 per share).

As this illustration makes clear, DRIPs are an easy way to grow your portfolio, and they're probably sounding like an easy decision. However, there are a few things you should know before you sign up. First, if you're investing for current income needs, you obviously can't use a DRIP. Next, even if you reinvest your dividends, you still have to report them as income and pay tax on them (unless they're in a retirement account); you'll have to use other resources to pay those taxes. Finally, note that DRIPs are not offered on all investments, so if this feature is important to you, ask before purchasing.

DRIP participation is automatic for 401(k)s and IRAs held by mutual fund companies. Also, mutual funds usually allow you to sign up on the fund application. However, you may need to ask to participate in a DRIP in the case of a non-retirement investment or a self-directed IRA (i.e., one in which a brokerage acts as custodian, but you make the investment decisions).

A final thought about DRIPs: if your risk tolerance is low, DRIPs can be an excellent way to turn a lower-risk income investment into something akin to a growth investment.

DOLLAR-COST AVERAGING

The price of most investments fluctuates regularly. *Dollar-cost averaging* allows you to minimize the impact of short-term price changes on your investments by purchasing fixed amounts of a particular security at regular intervals. It is, as its name implies, a way to build a portfolio while investing at an *average* price, instead of an unusually high one.

ILLUSTRATION

You invest $400 per month in the XYZ mutual fund. In July, XYZ sells for $20 per share, so you purchase 20 shares. In August, it is down to $16 per share, so your $400 allows you to purchase 25 shares. In September, it is back at $20, so you acquire another 20 shares. You now own 65 shares of the fund at an average cost of $18.54 per share. Had you invested all $1,200 in July, you would have owned only 60 shares at an average cost per share of $20.

In reality, it's equally possible over such a short period that the price fluctuations in the last illustration could have gone the other way, and you'd have come out slightly behind. Over the long-term, however, dollar-cost averaging smoothes out the wrinkles caused by short-term price fluctuations, minimizing the risk of investing in a security at an inopportune time.

The last illustration highlights the kind of automatic dollar-cost averaging that comes through periodic investing (e.g., through payroll deductions into your 401(k) plan). The strategy is also ideally suited for avoiding inopportune highs when investing a lump-sum.

ILLUSTRATION

You have $30,000 you wish to invest in XYZ fund. On July 1, XYZ sells for $20 per share. You could invest all $30,000, purchasing 1,500 shares. Or, using dollar-cost averaging, you could invest $5,000 per week that week and each of the following five weeks (six weeks total). Assume the price is $21 per share on week 2, $20 per share on week three, $19 per share on weeks four and five, and $20 per share on week six. Instead of acquiring 1,500 shares at an average cost of $20 per share, you have acquired 1,514 shares at an average cost of $19.83 per share.

In this illustration you came out 14 shares ahead by using dollar-cost averaging. More importantly, however, you avoided the risk that you could have invested the entire amount in week two, when your $30,000 would have yielded only 1,429 shares, leaving you a more significant 71 shares behind. Again, how the actual math shakes out depends on the nature of the price fluctuations for your particular investment, but, over time, dollar-cost averaging will protect you from unwittingly buying at a market high.

LADDERING

If you purchase income investments (bonds or certificates of deposit), you'll probably want to adopt a *laddering* strategy: staggering the maturity dates of your investments (like the rungs on a ladder) in order to minimize the interest rate and reinvestment risks.

ILLUSTRATION

You have $100,000 you wish to invest in Treasury bonds. On July 1, the bonds are yielding 6.5 percent. You could invest all $100,000 on that date. However, because you know the price of Treasury bonds fluctuates daily (the week before, the yield was 6.43 percent), you instead decide to purchase $10,000 worth of bonds in each of the next 10 weeks, ensuring that you aren't stung by going to the bond market on the wrong day.

If you were able to follow well the logic behind dollar cost averaging above, try thinking of laddering as a sort of dollar-income averaging. By staggering maturity dates, and in the process the interest rates your investments will bear, you can obtain a market-average interest rate, thereby ensuring that you don't invest or reinvest the bulk of your portfolio at an inopportune time. Laddering can be especially effective if you are investing for current income needs.

INDEX FUND INVESTING

An *index fund* is a mutual fund whose portfolio is invested in a way that seeks to match as closely as possible the securities that comprise a particular benchmark index; many index funds, for example, tie their portfolios to the securities that constitute the S&P 500.

Some financial planners believe that most people should limit their investments to index funds. They raise several excellent points in support of their position. First, because index funds essentially match overall market performance, investors have a higher assurance that their portfolio will not lag behind. Similarly, most investors do not have the time or resources to make appropriate investment decisions on their own, so index funds offer peace of mind. Third, since the components of the index an index fund matches change little over time, the fund does not require active management; the fees and expenses associated with index funds are lower, allowing you to keep more of what you earn.

On the other hand, by limiting your investments to index funds, you necessarily preclude the possibility of above-market returns. Some mutual funds outperform others, and some stocks outperform the market. If you seek (or require) superior returns, you can't get them through index funds.

True, counters the first camp, but it's very hard for average investors to identify the securities that offer such superior returns. In fact, they continue, it's very hard for anybody to identify them; in 1996, for example, over 70 percent of mutual funds were unable to outperform the S&P 500. Since the star performers are so hard to identify, and since market returns are adequate for most investment goals, stick to index funds and get on with your life, they conclude.

Who to believe? A difficult decision, to be sure; index fund advocates offer compelling arguments, but their counterparts wield the ultimate trump card: the allure of superior returns. Index fund investing clearly makes sense in at least three situations: (1) when you're young and/or new to investing; (2) when you have a limited number of investment options (as with some 401(k)s); and, (3) when you are concerned that your overall portfolio is not sufficiently diversified. Beyond these, it is up to you to weigh the arguments pro and con to determine which is more consistent with your own investment philosophy.

SOCIALLY-RESPONSIBLE INVESTING

Lesbian and gay investors sometimes wonder whether their hard-earned dollars are being invested in companies that support or oppose the community and their civil rights. The follow-up question usually involves whether they should make community support a criterion in their investment decision-making. It's an important question of course, and one not always easily answered.

The issue is a subset of the larger trend to invest in companies that adopt certain socially-responsible business practices: environmental protection, worker safety, human rights, animal protection, no involvement in the production of nuclear technologies or tobacco products, and so on. There are several families of mutual funds that use a variety of these social "screens" in choosing investments. There is even one that screens solely on the basis of whether a company has adopted an employment non-discrimination policy with respect to sexual orientation.

Proponents of socially-responsible investing maintain that using social screens actually makes good business sense. Companies whose management is enlightened about, for example, lesbian and gay issues tend to be enlightened in all aspects of their decision-making; in theory, this should translate into superior performance. This sometimes happens; in fact, through most of 1997, several investment advisors who manage private portfolios using sophisticated screens on issues important to the lesbian and gay community report outperforming the market by more than 35 percent.

Unfortunately, not all socially-responsible investments can boast such returns. In fact, the returns from many socially-responsible mutual funds have been nothing less than disappointing. Thus, you must evaluate a socially-responsible investment the same as you would any other; if it is not performing adequately, it has no place in your portfolio. Regardless of how strongly you feel about corporate social responsibility, you cannot afford to invest for inferior returns.

For some people, investing is about risk and return—no more and no less; questions about corporate social responsibility never even enter the picture. For others, social responsibility is essential to deciding where they put their money. Many lesbian and gay investors find themselves somewhere in the muddled middle, wanting to do the right thing, but unsure of the risks involved. If you find yourself in this last category, perhaps you could try using social criteria as a "final check" before choosing between two otherwise appropriate investments.

If investing in companies that support the rights of its lesbian and gay workers, and the lesbian and gay community, is important to you, there are a limited number of avenues you can pursue to get the information you need to make socially responsible investment decisions. First, you can try to find information about which companies meet these criteria; organizations such as the Human Rights Campaign (whose Web site can be found at http://www.hrc.org) keep lists. Alternatively, you can seek out investment advisors or portfolio managers who track such issues; there are one or two in most major cities. Or you could seek out a mutual fund whose social policies are consistent with your views. With any of these options, however, be sure to carefully investigate performance history before investing; social responsibility cannot compensate for sub-standard returns.

A final thought about social investing: if this is a critical concern for you, be sure you understand which social screens you require, and be sure your investments meet those needs. It is one thing for a company to adopt a non-discrimination policy, for example; it is quite another for it to spend money on domestic partner benefits. Some companies are very philanthropic toward lesbian and gay community organizations. If you wish to set the bar very high on social issues, you'll need to spend a lot more time gathering information about potential investments. Of course, the higher you set the bar, the fewer investments you'll have to choose from—so, for one last time, don't compromise on the issues of diversification and return in the process of your social screening.

HOT TIPS AND MARKET TIMING

You've now worked through four chapters worth of information explaining how to perform investment planning to achieve your goals. As you reflect on what you've read, it may strike you as odd that there was no discussion of how to ferret out hot stock tips or to know when to anticipate a change in the market in order to make a killing. There's a good reason for that: these strategies won't work for you. In fact, if you're an average investor, you're likely to come out behind if you try to rely on them. There are (at least) two reasons for this:

First, recall the information from the last chapter explaining the role asset allocation plays in portfolio performance: 90 percent+ of the variation in a portfolio's performance was determined by whether or not it employed a proper asset allocation strategy, leaving 9 percent determined by all other factors. Market timing *is* one of those other factors, which suggests it wouldn't matter much even if you could get it right.

Moreover, only people who track investments 24/7—or who can afford to pay others to do so—can amass the information necessary to successfully time the market. Hot tips and market timing are likely to leave average investors the proverbial day late and dollar short. Think about it for a moment: by the time you pick up on what sounds like a hot tip, don't you suppose that the people who earn their livelihood managing investments have already heard about it—and taken advantage of it? Just what does that leave for you? You should always invest for the long-term. Hot tips and market timing are better left to the professional investors—including mutual fund managers—who know how to work them.

PART IV

Preparing for the Unexpected: Insurance Planning

CHAPTER 10

How to Use Life Insurance

Insuring against the risk of financial ruin in the event of your untimely death is a basic tool of financial planning. Life insurance also can be a cost-effective way to meet financial planning goals. Use the checklist below to see which uses of life insurance may be appropriate for you.

FIGURE 10-1
LIFE INSURANCE USES CHECKLIST

_____ Provide a replacement income stream to help a partner or dependent family member maintain his or her standard of living

_____ Pay off mortgages, loans, and other debts

_____ Pay federal estate taxes

_____ Pay state inheritance taxes

_____ Provide beneficiaries with ready access to cash while an estate is being administered

_____ Make charitable contributions

_____ Buy out the interest of a deceased business partner

_____ Provide protection to business from loss of a key employee

_____ Pay for funeral expenses

_____ Provide tax-advantaged investing

The type of risk you are insuring against will dictate the amount of insurance you purchase. For example, you can determine with some certainty your funeral costs or state inheritance taxes, and purchase a corresponding amount of life insurance. On the other hand, if you want to insure against the loss of an income stream, determining how much insurance to buy may not be easy. You might consult with a financial planner in order to account for all of the variables that need to be considered in determining the amount of insurance needed to replace that income stream. However, a very rough rule of thumb is to multiply the annual need by 7 in order to determine your life insurance needs; if you are very young, or you have a very high income, you might consider raising that multiple as high as 10.

ILLUSTRATION

Roni and Jeri own a home in the city together. They also own a vacation home in the mountains. The mortgage on the city house is $200,000 and the vacation home is $100,000. Together they can afford both mortgage payments, but if something should happen to one of them the survivor could not afford to make both payments. They each take out an insurance policy for $300,000 so that the survivor can use the funds to pay off the mortgages.

ILLUSTRATION

Tom is the sole breadwinner for his household, earning $100,000 per year. His partner Kurt maintains the house and organizes all social activities. Kurt receives a small income from a trust fund established by his grandfather. Tom is concerned that if anything should happen to him, Kurt would not be able to maintain his lifestyle. Tom consults a financial planner. After taking into account his assets, liabilities, investments, Kurt's age, and his trust income, it is determined that the amount of cash needed to replace the lost income stream for Kurt's life would be $750,000.

There are two fundamental categories of life insurance: *term insurance* and *cash value insurance.* Term insurance simply pays a death benefit, while cash value insurance both pays a death benefit and offers a tax-deferred savings feature. There are different types of both term and cash value insurance, each suited to different needs.

TERM INSURANCE

Term insurance provides protection for a specified time period. If you die during the term, your beneficiaries collect the death benefit. If you live to the end of the term, you must either renew the policy (if eligible) or your relationship with the insurer ends. Term insurance costs less than cash value insurance because it provides only death protection.

ILLUSTRATION

Mark has a son from a former marriage who is 11 years old. Mark wants to make sure that if anything should happen to himself there are adequate funds to pay for his son's college education. He estimates that it will cost $100,000 for tuition and expenses for four years. Mark purchases a term life insurance policy for $100,000 that expires when his son turns 25.

There are two types of term life insurance. You can purchase a *level premium* policy for a set period of years or you can buy an *annual renewable* policy, in which the premium increases each year. Level premium term usually costs less than an annual renewable policy over the long-run. Thus, for short-term needs, annual renewable may be more appropriate. If you opt for annual renewable, make sure your policy contains a renewability clause so that your insurer cannot cancel (technically, refuse to renew) the policy.

ILLUSTRATION

Same facts as the last illustration. A level premium policy for fifteen years costs $95 per month. An annual renewable policy costs $60 per month for the first year with the premium increasing 3 percent per year. Mark chooses the annual renewable policy.

CASH VALUE INSURANCE

The attractive feature of cash value insurance is its ability to accumulate savings, or a cash value, in addition to the death benefit of the policy. The savings grow tax-deferred, allowing some forms of cash value insurance to serve as an attractive investment vehicle. If you terminate, or cash-in, the policy early, you receive the accumulated cash benefit less a small redemption fee. By contrast, with term insurance, if you cancel the policy you receive nothing. Of course, premiums for cash value insurance are higher than for term insurance.

Policy Loans. You can borrow against the accumulated savings in a cash value policy, usually at attractive interest rates. This offers a handy alternative to high-interest rate credit cards in the event of a sudden cash crunch. You should only use this feature in emergencies or as a debt management tool of last resort. All policy loans are subtracted from the death benefit if you should die before paying off the loan.

Surrendering a Policy. If at some future time you decide to stop making premium payments on your policy, there usually are three options for the cash built-up in the policy. First, you can withdraw the cash and pay income tax on a portion of the build-up. Second, you can use the cash value to buy a fully "paid-up" insurance policy. In essence you are using the cash value to buy a policy through a one-time premium payment. The death benefit of the new policy will be lower than the policy you are giving up, but will be permanent. The death benefit is based on the amount of your cash value. The third option is to use the cash value to buy term insurance at the company's then-prevailing rates. You buy an amount of term coverage providing the same death benefit as your old cash value policy. The coverage lasts for as long as your cash value can pay for the premiums. This differs from the second option where you get a permanent coverage with a lower death benefit; here the death benefit is unchanged from the original policy, but the coverage lasts for a shorter period.

There are four major types of cash value insurance available: (1) whole life, (2) universal life, (3) variable life, and (4) variable universal life.

1. **Whole life** is the most conservative form of cash value insurance. Premiums usually remain the same during the length of the policy.

There are no investment options for the savings portion of the premium. The insurance company makes all investment decisions, which tend to be conservative, so the rate of return on the accumulated savings is low.

2. **Universal life** provides more flexibility than whole life. It was designed to allow policyholders to adjust all the major features of an insurance policy to meet their changing financial needs: the premium payment, death benefit, and cash value build-up. You can use part of the accumulated cash value build-up to pay part or all of the premiums. You also have the option of changing the amount of the death benefit of the policy. Since the insurance company has higher administrative costs by giving you this flexibility, the policy premiums are higher than whole life. When a universal life policy is written, the insurance company assumes what interest rates the cash value portion of the policy will earn. If those assumptions are wrong, you may have to pay additional premiums in order to continue funding the same death benefit. Like whole life insurance, the insurance company makes all investment decisions for you with universal life.

3. **Variable life** is similar to whole life, but with one important difference: you make the investment decisions for the built-up cash value. The premium does not change and the death benefit is guaranteed. The cash value portion of the policy changes with the performance of the investments you choose. You invest the cash build-up in a family of mutual funds associated with or managed by the life insurance company writing the policy. Therefore, in selecting a variable life policy, it is important that you check not only the insurance company's performance but also the performance of the funds they manage. If the fund selection is limited or fund performance is below average, you could defeat your goal of tax-deferred investing.

4. **Variable universal life** combines the flexibility features of universal life with the investment options of variable life. This is high-powered insurance, suitable only for those who understand the intricacies of both insurance and investing, or whose portfolios are large enough to justify paying for that type of advice.

WHICH IS BETTER: TERM OR CASH VALUE?

The type of life insurance you purchase, of course, should be based on your needs: why you are buying life insurance, how long you need the insurance, and your ability to afford the premiums. If your need for insurance is only short-term, then term insurance may be more appropriate. Term insurance policies also are well-suited to business, charitable, and estate planning uses of life insurance.

On the other hand, cash value insurance may be better suited to long-term needs. Also, the tax advantages of cash value insurance as an investment vehicle may be attractive if you are in a high tax bracket. Before using insurance as an investment, however, first be sure you are maxing out on contributions to tax-advantaged retirement plans (401(k)s, IRAs), and that you can commit to regular premium payments over an extended period.

Many financial planners believe that life insurance is an inferior investment, and that you are better off buying a term life policy, with its lower premiums, and investing your money elsewhere. However, both the "forced savings" aspect of cash value insurance and its tax advantages can be valuable to some people. Use your needs, timeframe, and ability to pay to decide which type of insurance is best for you.

If you are young and want to maximize the death benefit coverage from your insurance dollar, term insurance probably is a better choice. However, make sure that your term policy inlcudes a provision allowing you to convert it to a cash value policy if you decide further down the road that you prefer the advantages of cash value insurance.

BUYING LIFE INSURANCE

When you contact a life insurance agent or broker to buy insurance, he or she will present you with a *policy illustration*. The *policy illustration* contains all of the assumptions and projections made by the insurance company with regard to how it expects your policy to perform. Review it carefully and make sure the following information is included:

FIGURE 10-2
LIFE INSURANCE POLICY ILLUSTRATIONS CHECKLIST

_____ Assumes coverage through age 95

_____ Uses a reasonable interest rate assumption

_____ Uses a reasonable inflation rate assumption

_____ Correctly states your age, health, and smoking status

_____ Contains a renewability provision (for term insurance)

_____ Contains a conversion feature (for term insurance)

_____ Provides adequate investment options (for variable life and variable universal life)

If you are comparison shopping for insurance, make certain that the illustrations from competing insurers contain the same exact assumptions. A higher interest rate or coverage through a lower age will have a significant impact on the cost of the insurance. Don't focus on just the premium price; many important details can be buried in the fine print.

Always review the financial condition of any insurance company you plan to do business with. If an insurer were to go out of business, you risk loss of coverage, nonpayment of claims, or inability to obtain replacement insurance (you may become uninsurable or a higher risk after your old policy goes into effect). You minimize these risks by dealing only with highly rated companies. Several private companies rate insurance companies; Moody's, A.M. Best, and Standard and Poor's are the leaders in the rating field. Most libraries subscribe to one or more of these services, and some of them provide information over the Internet. If possible, work only with insurers that have received the highest rating from all three companies.

An insurance company's size and how long its has been in business also are important factors to consider. Be sure to find out how long the company has been writing the particular type of insurance you are buying. If this is a new line of business for the insurer, it may lack the experience needed to accurately set prices.

SPECIAL CONCERNS FOR THE GAY COMMUNITY

Accelerated Death Benefits (Viatical Settlements). By now, most members of the gay community are familiar with the concept of viaticating an insurance policy. The strategy gained widespread use as people living with AIDS struggled to meet their financial obligations, although it can be used with any life-threatening illness. Viatification can take one of two forms. Under the first, a person with a terminal illness irrevocably designates a viatical settlement company as beneficiary on his or her life insurance policy, in exchange for a payment equal to a percentage of the eventual death benefit. The payment can be comparatively low, sometimes only 50% or 60% of the death benefit. For a variety of reasons, insurance companies disliked the practices of viatical settlement companies, and began incorporating a second form of viatification known as "accelerated death benefits" into their policy contracts. Most policies now contain such a feature.

For several years, the tax treatment of viatical settlement payments was unclear. However, since January 1, 1997, payments made on a life insurance policy in anticipation of death are no longer subject to income tax.

Ironically, with the increasing efficacy of protease inhibitors and other drug therapies, many viatical settlement companies have begun to re-think their approach to viaticating the life insurance of people with HIV infection. Nevertheless, for people who are facing death, viaticating a life insurance policy is an important option for obtaining financial peace of mind at a time of crisis.

Gay Couples and Insurable Interests. When you apply for insurance, you are required to list your intended beneficiary on the application. The insurance company may refuse to accept your proposed beneficiary if he or she does not have an *insurable interest* in your life. An insurable interest is one in which the beneficiary has a vested interest in your life and would suffer a recognizable financial loss from your death. Usually a spouse, children, parents, blood relatives, charities, or business partners qualify. For lesbian and gay couples, insurance companies historically have assumed that there is no insurable interest in each other's lives.

There is one small exception to this traditional rule: lesbian and gay couples who own a house together have an insurable interest in each other up to the amount of their share of the mortgage. This is akin to the logic used for two unrelated business owners who purchase coverage on each other's lives, but only up to the amount of the economic loss they'd suffer if their co-owner died unexpectedly.

There are ways to work around this problem. First, some insurance companies are beginning to recognize lesbian and gay partners as having insurable interests in each other's lives. A knowledgeable insurance agent or financial planner can tell you which companies are doing this in your area. Seek these companies out—they deserve community support for their efforts. Second, an agent or broker with experience serving the lesbian and gay community may be in a position to work with the underwriters in an insurance company's home office to avoid this problem. Finally, if neither of these options is available to you, name a parent or sibling as the beneficiary on your application. After a few months you can change the beneficiary to your partner. Although this is a game insurance companies dislike, it is largely of their own making, and entirely within their ability to eliminate.

CHAPTER 11

Disability Insurance

T he ability to earn a living is an asset that most people take for granted. If you are young and in good health, it's unlikely you've given much thought toward what would happen if you were suddenly to become disabled. Nevertheless, studies show that, at age 35, an individual faces a one-in-three chance of experiencing total disability for up to three months before age 65, with 30 percent of those cases resulting in permanent disability. At age 35, disability poses a greater risk for you than any other hazard, including death.

Usually, you'll need to replace between 60 percent and 70 percent of your income in the event a disability leaves you unable to earn a living. While some expenses go down when you can no longer work, such as clothing and transportation, others go up, such as food and medical care. Moreover, most expenses continue regardless of a disability, and these tend to be the major ones, such as housing and utilities.

For most people, the financial consequences from a serious disruption in income due to disability are enormous. Moreover, the benefits from workers' comp and Social Security do not provide adequate replacement for lost income, are too difficult to qualify for, or restrict coverage to only certain injuries. Clearly, with risks this high, insurance is the appropriate risk management technique to protect yourself from financial loss in the event of your disability.

Many people receive disability insurance coverage as a fringe benefit from their employers. If you do, you may want to compare the coverage provided against the criteria in the checklist below to see if it is adequate.

FIGURE 11-1

WHAT TO LOOK FOR IN A DISABILITY INSURANCE POLICY

_____ *Amount of Coverage.* Your policy should replace between 60% and 70% of your pre-disability income.

_____ *Definition of Disability.* Make sure your policy does not exclude coverage for "occupational" disabilities (i.e., those that arise on the job and for which you receive workers' compensation benefits).

_____ *Definition of Occupation.* Some policies provide coverage as soon as a disability prevents you from continuing to work in your *own occupation*; others require you to be unfit for work in *any occupation* before benefits are paid. The latter is unacceptable. If you can't find permanent "own occ" coverage, your policy should at least offer own occ benefits for the first five to ten years before switching to an "any occ" definition.

_____ *Renewability.* In order to avoid the risk that your insurer could refuse to renew your policy at a time when you would be unable to obtain replacement coverage, make sure your insurance is *noncancellable* or *guaranteed renewable*. You may be offered other types of renewability provisions, but they are inadequate.

_____ *Waiting Period.* This refers to how long you have to wait after becoming disabled before benefits begin to be paid. 90 days is standard, but with individual coverage you can choose a longer waiting period in order to lower your premium.

_____ *Inflation.* Your policy should include a cost-of-living adjustment so that any benefit payments that last over an extended period can keep pace with inflation.

_____ *Waiver of Premium.* Unless your policy includes a provision waiving the continued payment of insurance premiums in the event of a disability, you would have to use part of your disability benefits to keep up the premium payments on your policy.

_____ *Definition of Illness.* Make sure your policy covers illnesses when they are *first manifest*, not when they are first contracted or *begin*. With the latter, benefits can be denied for an illness contracted before the policy begins—even if its existence is unknown. This could be devastating for illnesses with long dormant periods like HIV or cancer.

There are many types of coverage available, so you can't assume your employer's plan is a good one. If there are gaps in your employer's plan, you should consider buying supplemental coverage; sometimes you can even do this through work. If not, consider purchasing coverage on your own.

If you don't have disability insurance coverage, there is a serious gap in your financial planning; you should purchase a policy as soon as possible. When evaluating a potential policy, use the checklist above to ensure you're getting all you need. Also be sure to check out the insurance company offering the coverage, using the same criteria outlined for life insurers in the last chapter.

For lesbians and gay men, disability coverage takes on added importance because the expenses associated with disability may be higher than average. If you are geographically or emotionally isolated from your biological family, the support usually forthcoming in the event of a crisis, such as disability, is not likely to be there. Without that support, you may have to pay for even routine household assistance. While the additional exposure potentially exists for everyone in the community, it is particularly acute for non-coupled lesbian and gay men, making the need for disability coverage even more urgent.

CHAPTER 12

Insuring Your Property

People who own property need to insure against several types of loss: theft or destruction of the property, loss of use of the property, and damage caused to others or to property owned by others. For most people, the two biggest assets presenting various permutations of these risks are their homes (and the things in them) and their cars. To adequately insure against the financial risk associated with these assets, you need to know what to look for in insurance policies.

HOMEOWNER'S INSURANCE

There are seven types of risk homeowner's insurance protects against: (1) damage to your house; (2) damage to other structures (e.g., a detached garage); (3) damage to personal property; (4) expenses from an inability to use damaged property; (5) medical expenses for injuries to others; (6) legal liability for injuries to others; and, (7) damage to property of others.

Your homeowner's policy should insure against each of these risks, and most do. Once you are sure that the policy covers all of the risks listed above, make sure that it also contains the features in the checklist below. You can use this list both when shopping for a new policy and when reviewing the adequacy of your current coverage.

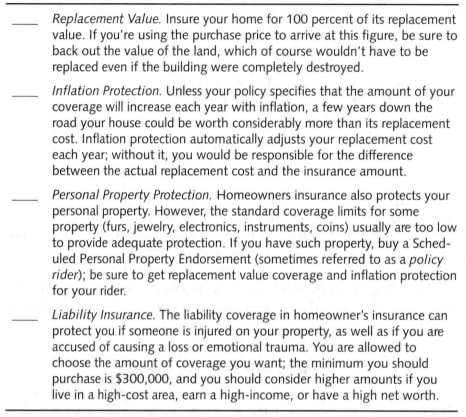

FIGURE 12-1
WHAT TO LOOK FOR IN A HOMEOWNER'S POLICY

_____ *Replacement Value.* Insure your home for 100 percent of its replacement value. If you're using the purchase price to arrive at this figure, be sure to back out the value of the land, which of course wouldn't have to be replaced even if the building were completely destroyed.

_____ *Inflation Protection.* Unless your policy specifies that the amount of your coverage will increase each year with inflation, a few years down the road your house could be worth considerably more than its replacement cost. Inflation protection automatically adjusts your replacement cost each year; without it, you would be responsible for the difference between the actual replacement cost and the insurance amount.

_____ *Personal Property Protection.* Homeowners insurance also protects your personal property. However, the standard coverage limits for some property (furs, jewelry, electronics, instruments, coins) usually are too low to provide adequate protection. If you have such property, buy a Scheduled Personal Property Endorsement (sometimes referred to as a *policy rider*); be sure to get replacement value coverage and inflation protection for your rider.

_____ *Liability Insurance.* The liability coverage in homeowner's insurance can protect you if someone is injured on your property, as well as if you are accused of causing a loss or emotional trauma. You are allowed to choose the amount of coverage you want; the minimum you should purchase is $300,000, and you should consider higher amounts if you live in a high-cost area, earn a high-income, or have a high net worth.

Documenting Personal Property. In order to prove the amount and value of your personal property, make an inventory of it. You might even consider using a video camera to make a "walking tour" of your home for this purpose. Store the inventory, along with receipts for big-ticket items, in a safe, fire-proof location. Update your inventory every couple of years.

Condominium Owner's Insurance. If you own a condominium, your homeowner's association insures the common elements, including the building itself. However, you are personally responsible for the contents of your own unit. This not only includes your personal property, but the interior walls, fixtures, electrical systems, and so on. For example, if a fire destroys your bathroom, you not only will have to replace all your towels, but the cabinet or closet that holds them, the vanity, sink, bathtub and commode. If the fire destroys a wall between your bathroom and bedroom, you will have to rebuild the wall and everything inside it (wiring, plumbing). Moreover, your condo association's master policy will not protect you from liability for injuries to others inside your unit. If you own a condo, you need condo owner's insurance; use the checklist above to be certain you have adequate coverage.

Renter's Insurance. Renters find themselves in a situation similar to that of condo owners: although the landlord is responsible for some of the seven risks outlined earlier in this chapter, the tenant remains responsible for others. While fixtures and interior walls are not a tenant's responsibility, personal property and liability for injuries to others are. Renter's insurance protects against these risks, and usually is very reasonably priced; it is an essential component of proper financial planning. Use the applicable portions of the checklist above to be certain you have adequate coverage.

Partners and Other Unmarried Cohabitants. There is an important trap that can arise for partners and other roommates in gay households: anybody whose name is not on the deed to the house may not be covered under the homeowner's policy. Thus, if only one partner owns the couple's residence, or if a homeowner has housemates, the non-owners may need to obtain renter's insurance, and of course should do so. Only your insurance agent or broker can tell you if you face this problem. However, be sure you are working with a knowledgeable broker and be certain he or she has specifically investigated your concern—even good agents miss this one!

AUTOMOBILE INSURANCE

There are three types of risk associated with owning and operating a car: (1) legal liability to others; (2) physical injury to yourself or other occupants in the automobile; and, (3) damage to or loss of your vehicle. In order to insure adequately against the losses that can arise from these risks, use the checklist below to evaluate new or existing policies.

FIGURE 12-2
WHAT TO LOOK FOR IN AN AUTO INSURANCE POLICY

_____   *Liability Protection.* Most state laws impose minimum requirements for purchasing liability protection; unfortunately, these laws generally only require around $25,000 in coverage—a totally inadequate figure in the event of a serious accident and the lawsuits guaranteed to follow it. You should obtain at least $300,000 in liability protection, and consider even more if you live in a high-cost area, earn a high income, or have a high net worth.

_____   *Physical Injury (Medical Payments).* This coverage pays for the medical expenses incurred by occupants of the car (and any pedestrians you may hit) resulting from an accident. Standard coverage is $1,000 per person, but you should opt for $5,000 or even $10,000. Medical payment coverage is coordinated with any health insurance coverage.

_____   *Physical Damage to the Vehicle.* Coverage for damage to your car contains two components: collision (when your car collides with another object) and comprehensive (from any other cause—e.g., pebbles hitting the windshield, thieves smashing a window). You can choose the deductible for this coverage, and higher deductibles can lower your premiums. Note, too, that you can have different deductibles for collision and comprehensive.

_____   *Loss of Use.* For an extra fee, you often can obtain coverage that reimburses you for all or part of the fees you would pay to rent a replacement car while yours in being repaired or replaced. If the extra cost is nominal, the coverage may be worth it; otherwise, you're probably better off self-insuring.

_____   *Uninsured Motorist Coverage.* Most state laws require you to carry coverage in the event you are hit by an uninsured driver. As with basic liability protection, the amount required usually is too low; you should obtain uninsured motorist coverage limits equal to the limits you've chosen for your basic coverage.

_____   *Underinsured Motorist Coverage.* A risk that does not receive the consideration it deserves: what would happen if you were hit by a motorist who has bought only the legal minimum amount of insurance? The driver has insurance, so your uninsured motorist coverage would not apply; nevertheless, the other driver's coverage probably won't compensate you adequately in the event of a serious accident. You can obtain this optional insurance when you increase the limits on your uninsured motorist coverage; again, you should opt for the same limits you've chosen for your basic coverage.

Reducing Your Car Insurance Cost

Several factors influence the cost of your automobile insurance: where you live; where you drive; your age, gender, and marital status; whether your car is used for commuting, pleasure, or business; your driving record; the other business you do with the same insurer; safety features like airbags, anti-lock brakes, and anti-theft devices; your deductible; and, your coverage amount. To make sure you are getting the best price for the coverage you desire, consider the tips on page 104.

Gay Couples and Car Ownership

As you'll learn in the next chapter, joint ownership of property can be a very useful estate planning tool. However, cars present an important exception to this rule. The liability risks associated with joint car ownership far outweigh the estate planning benefits. Think of it this way: a car is a mobile invitation to be sued. Why expose two individuals to this risk if you don't have to?

Many auto insurers will not issue joint coverage for unmarried people who own a car together. Although this is slowly changing, you could end up paying more in insurance if you both have to take out separate policies. If you find yourself in this situation, make sure both policies contain the same coverage.

Another reason joint ownership can be a bad idea for gay couples: in most places, insurance premiums cost more. Traditionally, auto coverage was not designed for unmarried couples; each had to buy an individual policy, at a higher total cost than family coverage. While a few insurers have begun targeting coverage to gay couples, it is only available in a few geographic areas.

If, as recommended, only one partner owns the car, the other partner should be listed on the policy as an occasional driver. If one partner owns both cars, the non-owner partner should be listed as an occasional driver of the first car and the primary driver of the second car, with the owner listed as an occasional driver for the second car. These strategies will keep you on the up-and-up with your insurer so you aren't denied coverage in the event of an accident.

Whether you obtain a joint policy or list your partner as an occasional driver, read the fine print very carefully to be sure you both have identical coverage; occasionally, there are small but significant differences between the coverage afforded primary and occasional drivers (e.g., when renting a car). Work with a knowledgeable insurance agent or broker who has contacted the home office and read the fine print in your policy regarding these issues—even experienced agents have been known to miss details this minute.

FIGURE 12-3
SAVING ON CAR INSURANCE

_____ *Re-evaluate Physical Damage Coverage.* If your car is quite old and has a low book value, consider dropping the physical damage coverage from your policy. The insurance company won't reimburse in excess of the book value, so this may be a good place to self-insure.

_____ *Safety Devices.* Insurers often offer discounts for certain safety devices such as airbags, anti-lock brakes, and passive (automatic) arming car alarm systems. Make sure your insurer knows when you have these items.

_____ *Multi-car Discounts.* If you use the same insurer to cover all your cars, you usually can obtain a small discount.

_____ *Multiple Insurance Discounts.* If you use the same insurer for all your property coverage, you sometimes can obtain a small discount.

_____ *Commuting versus Pleasure Driving.* Your premium takes into account how many miles you drive and how many of those miles are for commuting (when the risk of accident is higher). If public transportation is available, consider taking it. If it is not available or is unreliable, consider carpooling. The rates for a pleasure car are lower than the rates for a commuting one. Keep track of the miles driven on each car and make sure your insurer uses accurate information in computing your premium.

_____ *Good Driving Discount.* Most insurers will reward you if you have no chargeable accidents (ones that were your fault) or traffic violations over a five-year period. If you qualify, make sure you are receiving this discount.

_____ *Defensive Driving Course.* Many insurers offer a discount if you attend an approved defensive driving course. Check with your insurer to see if they offer this discount—and take the course.

_____ *Watch Your Speed.* Moving violations (speeding tickets, running red lights, etc.) increase your insurance premium. Slow down and save some money—and perhaps your life.

PART V

Preparing for the Inevitable: Estate Planning

CHAPTER 13

Wills and Trusts

W hat happens to the property you own when you die? By law, it is transferred to other people in one of four ways:

1. Automatically through joint ownership;

2. By designation of a beneficiary;

3. Through a trust; and/or,

4. Under the probate laws.

If you don't arrange before your death for your property to transfer using one of the first three methods, it automatically becomes subject to the probate laws when you die. If you have a valid will when you die, the probate laws usually allow that to control who receives your property; if not, a state *intestacy* law makes the decisions for you.

It's not always a bad thing if your property is transferred under the probate laws, but there are a number of reasons you might want to avoid— or at least minimize—the probate process. This is especially true for lesbian and gay couples.

The probate laws in each state are intended to insure that your assets are transferred in an orderly and appropriate manner when you die. Most importantly, they're meant to assure that the people you want to receive your assets—or are most likely to want to receive them—actually do get them. And the process generally works well. However, it's not without its drawbacks.

For one thing, probate can take time. Since the process is subject to court supervision, and thus to a number of court filings, it may take several months before your estate can start distributing assets to your loved ones. This sometimes creates cash flow problems if survivors need access to your money to pay ongoing expenses—mortgages, car payments, utilities, and so on.

Next, the process is a very public one. Probate court proceedings are matters of public record. This means that anyone who wants to know your business is free to do so.

Moreover, there are fees associated with probate that can be avoided (or at least minimized) through proper planning. To be sure, the case for cost-savings associated with probate-avoidance (e.g., trusts) has been over-stated by the general media and by the aggressive marketing tactics of some estate planners. Nevertheless, there are better ways to spend money, and avoiding probate means avoiding the expenses associated with it—generally court costs and lawyer's fees.

Fourth, if you own real estate in another state, your probate problems can multiply. Although most assets are probated in the state where you live, real estate is probated in the state where it is located. If your vacation home is across state lines, your estate is facing a separate, second probate proceeding—referred to as *ancillary probate*.

Finally, for lesbian and gay couples, probate can add an extra layer of complexity and stress to the process of distributing a deceased partner's assets. A few experts have referred to probate as "a lawsuit you bring against yourself for the benefit of your creditors." For gay couples, it's also a lawsuit you bring against yourself for the benefit of your potentially hostile family members. If a family member decides not to abide by the wishes you've clearly expressed in your will, all they have to do is complain to the court. Remember, probate is a legal proceeding, and the judge has the authority to decide whether a complaint has merit. Also remember that the judge that hears a will contest may or may not have a frame of reference for understanding your relationship. While few wills are contested, and will contests usually fail, they are always expensive. The fees paid to defend a will challenge come from the estate's assets.

It's important not to allow yourself to be fooled into thinking this could "never happen" in your family. The death of a loved one is such an overpowering event, it can cause the best of people to do bizarre and unexpected things. No matter how well you think you know your family, and no matter how implicitly you trust them, and no matter how accepting they are of your partner, it is a certainty that your death will be devastating to them. How they will respond to the emotional overload caused by your death is anybody's guess. Are you prepared to leave your partner's chances in the hands of a person in such a frame of mind?

Of course, if you're already estranged from your biological family as a result of your sexual orientation, you understand clearly the need to avoid a court battle with them after you're gone. If you think you or your partner are at risk in this regard, the following checklist can help you plan to avoid a will challenge:

FIGURE 13-1
CHECKLIST FOR MINIMIZING
THE CHANCES OF A WILL CONTEST

_____ Use probate alternatives (joint property, beneficiary designations, revocable living trusts) to minimize the assets that will pass under your will.

_____ Mention all family members in your will, even if you do not wish to make a bequest to them.

_____ Include an _in terrorem_ clause in your will if it is valid in your state.

_____ If you are in a relationship, name your partner as your personal representative.

_____ If your health status is uncertain, prepare a will now to avoid any question of your "sound mind" later.

_____ Keep your will current, and obey all necessary formalities when executing your will. If you are in a relationship, be certain your partner is _not_ in the room when you execute your will (and vice versa).

_____ Provide at least one family member with complete details of your estate planning.

_____ Work with a professional who understands the unique estate planning challenges faced by lesbians and gay men.

As bad as all this may sound, it can get even worse. If you haven't clearly stated your wishes through a valid will, it is certain your surviving partner will lose out. Intestacy statutes vary by state, but there is a general pattern to how they work: first, the statute usually gives everything to a legal spouse (and provides for any minor children). If there's no spouse, the assets usually go to children; if there are no children, then to parents; if there's no parent, then to grandchildren; and so on. The rules are fixed and rigid, so there's no flexibility to provide for a best friend, a favorite nephew, or a respected charity. Most importantly, the intestacy laws that govern the transfer of probate property when someone dies without a will do not provide for domestic partners. Period. If you die without a will, in no circumstances will the law provide for your partner.

It's very unlikely your surviving family members will be able to work around the intestacy laws to provide for your surviving partner. The fact of your death may overwhelm your family and, for the reasons discussed above, you cannot rely on distraught people to keep their promises. Moreover, even if they were inclined to respect your wishes, the transfer by your family of any substantial amounts of money to your surviving partner undoubtedly would create gift tax problems. If "honoring your wishes" requires giving more than $10,000 per family member to your surviving partner, a gift tax return will have to be filed.

In summary, then, the estate planning strategies for lesbians and gay men are clear: avoid probate where it makes sense and under no circumstances allow yourself to die without a valid will.

WHAT'S IN A WILL?

A will, of course, is a legal document. Like most legal documents, it contains a number of standard clauses. You may find it helpful to be familiar with these clauses before you start planning your will.

> *Final Arrangements Clause.* In most states, there is a legal limit on the amount your estate can pay for your final arrangements, unless you specifically waive that limit in your will. If you don't include such a clause, your estate may not be able to pay for the type of funeral you've specified.

> *Residuary Clause.* Usually, after making all your specific bequests (e.g., "my collection of Elvis memorabilia to my nephew, Wes"), your will should include a residuary clause leaving the remainder of your assets to an individual, group of individuals, or charitable institution(s). The residuary clause makes sure none of your assets

"fall through the cracks." Note, however, that if your estate doesn't have enough assets to pay all its debts and make all its specific bequests, the beneficiaries named in the residuary clause usually are the first to lose their bequests.

Tax Clause. Under the laws in most states, any taxes owed by your estate are paid out of the residuary first. If you don't like this arrangement, you need to include a tax clause indicating where the money should come from.

Simultaneous Death Clause. What happens if your beneficiary dies at the same time you do? Do you still want your bequest to go to her, knowing that it's going to pass immediately to her beneficiaries under her will? A simultaneous death clause prevents this, and makes sure the property passes instead to the alternate beneficiaries you've named in your will.

In Terrorem Clause. An in terrorem clause stipulates that someone who challenges your will receives nothing. In some states, it's either difficult or impossible to persuade a court to enforce an in terrorem clause. In other states, it's perfectly legal to include one in your will. Properly used, in terrorem clauses may be a helpful strategy for lesbian and gay couples. If in terrorem clauses are valid in your state, they may be a way to discourage family members from challenging bequests to your surviving partner.

Disinheriting. Unless it's a minor child (and, in a few states, a surviving spouse), you are free to disinherit any family member you wish to. Although you can accomplish this simply by not making a bequest to the person you wish to disinherit, it's usually smarter to specifically include their name and your decision not to provide for them. Don't be spiteful, but don't hedge, either. A disinherited relative is a prime candidate for a will challenge, and you want your intentions to be clear to any judge asked to rule on them.

Appointment of Personal Representative. Although the court must approve the person you nominate as the personal representative of your estate, this is almost always a formality. Since state laws generally place severe restrictions on the powers granted to a personal representative (e.g., the types of investments he or she can make), your estate planner is likely to recommend including a broad list of additional powers in your will. Read the list carefully and mention any concerns, but broader powers generally give your personal representative needed flexibility in managing your estate. Specific considerations in choosing a personal representative are discussed later in this book. Note, however, that naming a surviving partner as your personal representative may give him or her additional leverage and authority in dealing with any hostile family members.

Codicil. A codicil is an economical alternative to executing a new will when you want to make only minor changes to your existing one. Note, however, that if the changes are extensive, or if you've already executed one or more codicils, it may be less confusing simply to draft a new will. A confusing trail of codicils can be an invitation to a will challenge.

THE PROBATE PROCESS

In order to begin the probate process, the person named in your will as your personal representative (also known as executor/executrix) must file a probate petition with the court. In the case of intestacy, courts generally appoint a close blood relative as your personal representative. This usually happens about 30 days after death. Although the probate process varies somewhat depending on where you live, a personal representative usually has to:

1. "Open" the estate by filing a petition for probate and to be appointed as its personal representative;

2. Apply for a taxpayer identification number from the Internal Revenue Service;

3. Notify anybody to whom the decedent owed money;

4. Notify anybody entitled to receive property under the will (or the intestacy statute);

5. Publish legal notices in newspapers;

6. Open a checking account for the estate;

7. Close the decedent's bank and brokerage accounts, and open accounts in the estate's name;

8. Obtain appraisals for the estate's real and personal property;

9. Prepare an inventory of the estate's assets and liabilities;

10. Collect any money owed to the decedent (e.g., outstanding debts, life insurance proceeds);

11. Sell assets as directed by the will and approved by the court;

12. File all required tax returns;

13. Pay any taxes due;

14. File an accounting with the court detailing all of the money and other property collected and disbursed;

15. Pay the decedent's debts and the expenses of administering the estate;

16. Distribute the assets of the estate, usually in accordance with the terms of the will; and,

17. File a final petition with the court to "close" the estate.

The process can take as little as six months, but usually requires one to two years to complete. In some states, there are procedures for informal probate or abbreviated probate that can speed things up when the dollar value of a decedent's assets is below a specified limit or when all of the beneficiaries are immediate family members.

After considering the time, energy, and expense these duties may entail, you can see why probate usually requires the assistance of a lawyer! Of course, his or her fees will add to the cost of transferring your assets when you die, often on the order of 3 percent to 10 percent of the value of your probate estate. This alone can be motivation enough to try to avoid probate.

Joint Ownership

Joint ownership is the first of three possible alternatives to probate. In order to understand how this technique works, you need to know there are four ways to own property, each with a unique set of characteristics:

1. Individually

2. As a tenant in common with one or more other people

3. As a joint tenant with a right of survivorship

4. As a tenant by the entirety with your spouse

Of these four methods, the one that can help gay couples plan around probate is the joint tenancy with right of survivorship (JTWROS). In a JTWROS, when one co-owner dies, the surviving co-owner automatically owns the entire property. No court proceeding is necessary to transfer title. The survivorship provision in the title document would even take precedence over a contradictory bequest of the property in the decedent's will. By contrast, when a tenant in common dies, his or her share of the property is distributed through probate; the co-owners only receive it if that's what the will or the intestacy statute requires. That's the importance of the "survivorship" part of JTWROS—it's what keeps property out of probate.

A home is the most common asset people own as joint tenants with right of survivorship. However, virtually any asset that requires a title document can be held JTWROS: cars, boats, bank accounts, stocks, bonds, or mutual funds.

There are a few things to know about using the JTWROS option. First, some states are reluctant to believe that two unrelated people could really mean to create survivorship rights in each other for their joint property. The language in the title document has to be very specific in these states. While many states recognize the unadorned designation "joint tenants" to establish the survivorship right, some require the complete "joint tenants with right of survivorship" in the title. Worse, a handful even require the cumbersome "joint tenants with right of survivorship and not as tenants in common". Be certain of the rules in your state, and insist that they be followed to the letter.

Next, it's remotely possible for joint tenants to convert their ownership to tenants in common. This usually happens when one person does something inconsistent with the JTWROS form of ownership, such as trying to sell their individual interest. In theory, a disgruntled family member could try to persuade a court that a deceased joint tenant converted his or her interest to a tenancy in common, thus destroying the co-owner's survivorship rights. These claims are very rare, and seldom succeed even when raised.

However, since a successful claim would place the property in probate, it can create headaches.

It's easy to avoid this problem, though. Include a provision in your will that: (1) reiterates your intention to create a JTWROS; and, (2) leaves the property to your co-owner if for any reason the survivorship right isn't recognized.

You also may create estate tax problems if you own an asset JTWROS. For example, sometimes your estate plan may require you and your partner to own an asset unequally in order to minimize the value of your taxable estate. Estate tax issues are discussed in the next chapter. Meanwhile, if you have estate tax problems, your estate planner can tell you whether or not you can take advantage of the JTWROS option.

Beneficiary Designations

Beneficiary designations are the second alternative to probate, but only for certain types of property. When you buy life insurance or open a retirement account, you're asked to name one or more beneficiaries who will receive the proceeds from the policy or account when you die. You also are allowed to name one or more contingent beneficiaries, in case your original beneficiaries die before you. If you don't name a beneficiary, or if all your beneficiaries die before you do, the proceeds are paid to your estate. There are adverse tax and other consequences to having your estate as a beneficiary, so always keep your beneficiary designations current, and never name your estate as a beneficiary.

Revocable Living Trusts

Different types of trusts serve different purposes. One of the most common trusts is the so-called revocable living trust, and it can serve as a powerful alternative to probate. In it's simplest form, here's how the strategy works: (1) create a revocable living trust; (2) name yourself and your partner, a friend, a family member, or trusted advisor as co-trustees; and, (3) transfer all your property into the trust. The trust document requires all of the trust's income to be paid out to you. Most importantly, the trust also specifies what happens to the trust property when you die. In fact, the bequest language in both wills and revocable trusts often sounds quite similar. Since the trust is revocable, there are no adverse income tax consequences. You still file income tax returns using your own name and Social Security number.

Who can benefit from revocable living trusts? Since the assets owned by a revocable living trust do not pass through probate, gay couples who want to avoid probate should give serious consideration to this strategy. Revocable living trusts also are ideal for avoiding ancillary probate of out-of-state property. There is one other advantage to a revocable living trust: if you become incapacitated, your co-trustee can act as a sort of attorney-in-fact for you, at least with respect to those assets owned by the trust. This power of attorney feature is an important consideration for gay couples.

With benefits like these, why doesn't everybody have a revocable living trust? There are several reasons. First, trusts cost more to set up than wills do. They also sometimes cost money to administer on an ongoing basis, especially if you choose a professional or institutional co-trustee. For a truly simple estate, it may not make sense to spend the extra money for a revocable living trust. Of course, trusts cost a lot less on the distribution end than probate does, so many people will come out ahead in the long run by using a revocable living trust.

One of the most important things to remember about revocable living trusts is that they require regular maintenance. All of your property has to be re-titled in the trust's name when you set it up, and you have to remember to title all new assets in the trust's name as you acquire them. Over time, most people forget to do this once in a while. Again, any asset that doesn't pass to your beneficiaries through your trust will have to go through probate. This means that a small lapse in trust maintenance could lead to huge unintended consequences. There's a simple solution to this risk, though: execute a *pour-over will,* giving any probate assets to the trust when you die. The trust then distributes the assets as if it owned them all along. In most states, this strategy ensures that your revocable living trust is 100% effective.

Note that there's one thing a revocable living trust *can't* do: save taxes. Because the trust is revocable, the tax law says you still own the property in it. If you own property, it's part of your estate for tax purposes, even if it isn't part of your estate for probate purposes. Thus, while a trust will save you probate fees, it will not save you any taxes. People often get confused on this, so don't let anybody tell you otherwise!

OTHER STRATEGIES WITH TRUSTS

In addition to revocable living trusts, there are some other common uses of trusts you should be aware of:

Estate Tax Planning. Certain types of trusts are important tools for minimizing estate taxes. These trusts usually take advantage of the fact that the tax law allows a deduction in computing estate taxes for property left to a spouse and for property left to a charity. These trusts are discussed in the next chapter.

Holding Property for Incapacitated Persons. People with serious mental, emotional, and/or physical disabilities may not be able to manage their own affairs. In this case, their assets often are placed in a trust and managed by a trustee.

Protecting Wealth. A spendthrift trust prevents a beneficiary from borrowing against the trust's assets or future income, and protects the trust from the beneficiary's creditors. This is a good way to protect beneficiaries who are irresponsible with money. Once income is paid out of the trust to the beneficiary, creditors have access to it. However, spendthrift trusts allow the trustee to decide whether, when, how much, or to whom to pay a beneficiary's share of the trust's income, making it easier to protect beneficiaries from themselves.

Owning Life Insurance. Irrevocable trusts can be used to remove the proceeds of a life insurance policy from someone's estate, or to hold a life insurance policy that is intended to pay the estate taxes of the person insured by the policy. These trusts are popular estate tax planning tools, and are discussed in detail in the next chapter.

Holding Property for Minors. Legally, minors cannot own property in their own names. Trusts therefore are an excellent way to hold and manage property for them. Trusts are not subject to the same investment restrictions as custodial accounts (i.e., Uniform Transfer to Minors Act (UTMA) accounts or Uniform Gifts to Minors Act (UGMA) accounts). In other words, trusts can invest in more aggressive assets than UGMA or UTMA accounts. More importantly, minors can claim the assets in a custodial account once they reach the age of majority, whereas the person setting up a trust determines the age at which its assets get distributed. Of course, trusts require both set-up and ongoing administration expenses, making them unattractive for nominal sums of money. Also, the income tax rates on a trust may be higher than the rates on a custodial account. You'll want to crunch the numbers before making a decision, but a trust is probably preferable if there's a substantial sum of money involved.

CHAPTER 14

Federal Estate Taxes

HOW THE ESTATE TAX WORKS

Although few Americans actually pay Federal estate taxes, a growing number have to plan to avoid them. Why? Because the estate tax is based on the value of *everything* you own when you die. The following table will give you some idea of how comprehensive the tax is:

FIGURE 14-1
ASSETS SUBJECT TO FEDERAL ESTATE TAX

Assets	Examples
Cash on Hand	Bank accounts (checking, savings, money markets, certificates of deposit)
Investments	Stocks, bonds, mutual funds
Retirement Accounts	IRAs, 401(k)s
Annuities	
Life Insurance	Death benefit on any policy you own
Debts Owing	Loans to family members, businesses
Small Businesses	Ownership of a proprietorship, partnership, corporation
Real Estate	Residences, investment property, raw land
Vehicles	Cars, boats, trailers

continues

(continued)

Assets	Examples
Personal Property	Clothing, jewelry, furs
Household Goods	Furniture, rugs, china, crystal, silver, artwork, electronics
Collections	Stamps, coins, guns

Now that you know *what* is taxed, you need to know *how much* of it you have to own before the tax kicks in. Currently, that threshold is $625,000; that is, you will owe tax on the amount of your taxable estate over $625,000. Note that Congress recently changed the law, and this figure, often referred to as the estate tax exemption, will increase gradually to $1 million by 2006. Note, too, that the real jumps in the amount of the exemption won't occur until 2004.

Estate tax rates start at 37 percent, and gradually increase to 55 percent (on estates over $3 million).

The tax law refers to your total assets as your *gross estate*. You are permitted to take certain deductions from your gross estate in order to arrive at your *taxable estate*. These deductions include:

1. Debts you owe when you die (e.g., a mortgage)

2. Expenses for administering your estate (e.g., lawyer fees)

3. Amounts you leave to your spouse (called the marital deduction)

4. Amounts you leave to charity (called the charitable deduction)

If you do a little quick math based on this information, you can see why estate tax planning is an issue for a growing number of people: a paid-off house, some life insurance, savings, and a 401(k), and you could be rapidly approaching that magical $625,000 mark.

If you are planning jointly with a partner, keep in mind that you need to worry about exceeding the exemption if your *combined* assets total that amount. Why? When the first one of you dies, the survivor usually is going to own most everything. Thus, even if the first death escapes tax, the second may not.

ILLUSTRATION

Your assets are worth $400,000, and your partner's are worth $350,000. If you were to die today, leaving the bulk of your estate to your partner, you would not owe any tax—your estate would be below the exemption amount. However, if your partner were to die a year later, he or she probably would owe substantial tax—the combined $750,000 estate is well over the current exemption amount.

You can use the following worksheet to assess your potential estate tax exposure:

FIGURE 14-2
DO YOU HAVE A FEDERAL ESTATE TAX PROBLEM?

Step One: Estimate Your Taxable Estate

Net Worth (or your combined net worth if you have a partner) from Your Balance Sheet	$_____
Death Benefits on Life Insurance You Own	$_____
Less: Charitable Bequests Upon Your Death	$_____
Estimated Taxable Estate:	$_____

Step Two: Assess Your Exposure

Is Your Estimated Taxable Estate Over $625,000?	Yes/No
Is Your Estimated Taxable Estate Near $625,000, and:	
You Own Assets that Will Appreciate Prior to Your Death?	Yes/No
You Expect to Live at Least Another 10 Years?	Yes/No
You Expect Any Significant Inheritances?	Yes/No

If you answered "yes" to any of the questions above, you may have a Federal estate tax problem, and will need to engage in some form of estate tax planning.

Working with an estate planning professional, there are strategies you can use to minimize or eliminate the estate tax bite, but they require advance planning.

GIFTS AND TAXES

The Federal estate tax is part of a larger transfer tax system designed to make sure that people don't use lifetime gifts to avoid taxes at death. Many years ago, Congress noticed that people were making deathbed gifts in order to reduce their taxable estates below the exemption amount. In effect, people were doing a last minute end-run around the system. In response, they created a "unified" estate and gift tax system. Under this system, a *taxable gift* has the effect of reducing the amount of your estate tax exemption.

What is a taxable gift? The law allows a $10,000 per donor per donee gift tax *annual exclusion*. That is, each year you may give $10,000 per person to as many people as you wish. Once you exceed $10,000 to any one person, the excess gift becomes taxable under the unified transfer tax system. Before actually paying any tax, however, you first reduce your estate tax exemption by the amount of the gift.

ILLUSTRATION

In 1998, you make a gift of $15,000 to your nephew, $5,000 in excess of the gift tax annual exclusion. Assuming you've made no other taxable gifts, your Federal estate tax exemption is reduced by a corresponding $5,000, from $625,000 to $620,000.

The gift tax presents a variety of challenges and planning opportunities. Many of these relate to estate tax planning, discussed below. Some are more directly related to the gift tax itself. Planned gifting strategies may be necessary to accomplish your goals without running afoul of the tax laws.

ILLUSTRATION

In the last illustration, you could have avoided any gift tax problems by giving half the amount to your nephew in December, and the other half in the following January.

Also, there's one important exception to the gift tax rules. Payments made to educational or health care institutions on behalf of another person do not count toward the $10,000 annual exclusion. The payment must be made directly to the institution; it cannot be transferred through the beneficiary. Also, in the case of educational institutions, the payments can only be made for tuition, not for room and board.

FEDERAL ESTATE TAX PLANNING STRATEGIES

At its most basic, the goal of estate tax planning is to reduce the value of your taxable estate below the exemption amount (currently $625,000), thereby eliminating any taxes. There are a number of planning strategies available to achieve this goal; the ones most important to lesbians and gay men are discussed below. Sometimes, too, circumstances combine to make it impossible to completely eliminate estate taxes; the use of life insurance in these instances also is discussed below.

Before digging in, however, it's worth making brief mention of one key estate planning strategy denied to lesbian and gay couples: the *marital deduction*. Under the Federal estate tax laws, a taxpayer is allowed to deduct from the value of his or her gross estate any amounts given to a spouse. A taxpayer who leaves a billion dollar estate to his wife won't owe a penny in estate taxes. Naturally, the wife's estate won't want to be stuck with the tax bill on a billion dollars, so the couple still has to engage in substantial estate planning.

Nevertheless, the unlimited marital deduction offers two important planning opportunities. First, it ensures that the payment of estate taxes won't impoverish a surviving spouse upon the first spouse's death. Since no tax is due on the assets left to the surviving spouse, he or she can be assured of maintaining the same standard of living enjoyed while the deceased spouse was alive. Second, the marital deduction has the effect of doubling the estate tax exemption, from the current $625,000 to $1.25 million.

ILLUSTRATION

Ralph and Donna Reed have assets worth $1.25 million. Ralph dies in 1998, leaving $625,000 to Donna and $625,000 to his two children. The bequest to Donna is not taxed because of the unlimited marital deduction. The bequest to his children is not taxed because it is not above the estate tax exemption amount. Ralph has transferred $1.25 million without paying any taxes.

Of course, in order to claim the marital deduction, one needs to be legally married.

ILLUSTRATION

Ralph and Donald Reed have assets worth $1.25 million. Ralph dies in 1998, leaving $625,000 to Donald and $625,000 to his two children. The bequest to Donald does not qualify for the marital deduction, but does count toward his estate tax exemption. The bequest to his children is subject to tax because he consumed his entire exemption on the gift to Donald. Ralph owes Federal estate taxes of $246,250.

The unavailability of the unlimited marital deduction to lesbian and gay couples creates unique challenges in planning to minimize estate taxes. It also means that couples with combined assets in excess of the exemption amount should take seriously the need for estate planning.

Three strategies are likely to come into play for lesbians and gay men who need to do estate tax planning, regardless of whether they are single or in relationships: gifting, charitable planning, and planning with life insurance.

Gifting

One sure-fire way to lower the value of your estate is to give away part of it to friends and loved ones. However, because of the overlap between the gift tax rules and the estate tax rules, using this strategy requires careful planning to avoid pitfalls.

The strategy works because you get a separate $10,000 gift tax annual exclusion for every person to whom you give money or other property. Thus, people with large families sometimes can solve their estate tax problems with just a few gifts.

ILLUSTRATION

Jamal, age 80, has two children and seven grandchildren. His estate is worth $700,000. By making a gift of $10,000 to all nine of his family members, he can reduce his estate to $610,000, below the 1998 estate tax exemption amount of $625,000. Jamal has solved his estate tax problem.

Some people find it necessary to adopt an annual gifting program in order to meet their estate tax planning objectives.

ILLUSTRATION

Same facts as in the last illustration, but assume Jamal's estate is worth $800,000. He will need to make annual gifts of $10,000 to his family members for each of the next two years in order to avoid estate tax.

Of course, too much of a good thing can be dangerous when it comes to annual gifting. If you go overboard on your gifting strategy, you may find yourself without sufficient resources to maintain your own standard of living. This problem can arise in either of two ways. First, you should be careful not to give away more than you will need to support yourself.

ILLUSTRATION

In the last illustration above, if Jamal had been 20 years younger, it may not have been wise to give away quite so much money. Jamal probably would need that money to support himself through many years of retirement.

Second, while it is important to keep an eye on your total assets, you also should be mindful of the impact of gifting on your liquidity and your cash flow.

ILLUSTRATION

Again, consider Jamal. If his assets consisted of a $300,000 house and a $200,000 vacation home, substantial gifts of cash would not be a wise strategy for him to pursue. It is unlikely that his remaining liquid assets would generate sufficient income to cover his living expenses.

The key then is to find the right balance between estate tax needs and cash flow needs.

ILLUSTRATION

Jamal could reduce the amount of his annual gifts from $10,000 to $5,000 in order to reduce the value of his estate and still provide a retirement income stream.

One final caution to keep in mind when developing a gifting strategy: while you can give away either cash or property, the latter requires some additional planning. The tax law provides a strong incentive for inheriting property that has appreciated substantially in value versus transferring it during the owner's lifetime. The reason: the built-in capital gains are cancelled on inherited property. By contrast, the gains transfer to the recipient in the case of a lifetime gift; a subsequent sale of such property will trigger capital gains tax.

ILLUSTRATION

You own stock worth $50,000. You bought the stock decades ago for $5,000. If you were to sell the stock, you would incur a capital gain of $45,000. If you were to give the stock to your niece, and she subsequently sold it, she still would incur a $45,000 capital gain. However, if you left the stock to her when you died, the $45,000 gain would be erased.

There are occasions when estate planners recommend gifting property. Usually they arise in the context of very large estates, and involve property that is expected to appreciate substantially in the future (stock in a family farm or business, real estate). Gifting property of any significant value therefore should be undertaken only after consulting with a knowledgeable professional.

Charitable Planning

Many people feel motivated to include charitable contributions as part of their estate planning. Fortunately, a number of planning techniques have evolved that allow people to achieve favorable estate tax results because of their generosity.

First, the tax laws allow you to deduct charitable contributions from the value of your estate before computing the estate tax. Thus amounts you leave to a qualified charity on your death reduce your estate tax bill. For those lesbians and gay men motivated to support the community through their estate planning, this technique alone can solve their tax problems.

ILLUSTRATION

> Consider Jamal from above one last time. If he were to leave $625,000 to his partner Etienne and the balance to the local gay men's health clinic, he would not owe any estate taxes.

Charitable bequests work well as an estate planning strategy for many lesbians and gay men. However, if the value of your estate is so high that you are unable to make the large contributions necessary to get below the estate tax exemption, your estate planner may recommend some form of charitable trust. There are three kinds of charitable trusts: two varieties of *charitable remainder trust* (CRT) and a *charitable lead trust* (CLT).

The CRT works like this: you place money or other property into a trust; the trust pays you income for a specified period of time or for your life, and upon your death gives the assets to the charity named in the trust. Since you no longer own the property in the trust, it is not part of your gross estate when you die. (Note that you may still owe income tax on the trust income if it comes from taxable investments.) The CLT merely reverses the sequence of events: the income stream goes to the charity while you're alive, and upon your death the assets go to the individuals you name in the trust as beneficiaries.

Charitable trusts offer another important benefit, too: an immediate income tax deduction for the value of the charitable contribution made by your trust. The amount of the deduction requires some higher-order number crunching best left to your estate planner, but basically involves assigning an actuarial value to the charity's interest in the trust.

There is one final charitable planning technique you may need to consider: the *pooled income fund* (PIF). A PIF is a common investment fund established by a charity. You make a (sizeable) contribution to the charity's PIF, and in return the PIF provides you with an income stream, either for life or for a fixed number of years. The strategy allows you to reduce your estate while retaining some cash flow. Again, your contribution will generate a partial income tax deduction. PIFs are expensive to establish and maintain, so it's usually only large charities (e.g., universities, museums) that offer them.

Planning With Life Insurance

Sometimes, it just isn't possible to whittle your assets down below the estate tax exemption amount using the available planning strategies. Perhaps you cannot or do not wish to gift away a portion of your estate, or perhaps your estate is simply too large for gifting and charitable planning strategies to be completely successful. Whatever the reason, there is one final fail-safe strategy you can use to minimize estate taxes: buy life insurance.

Here's how the strategy works: you and your planner estimate the amount of the estate taxes you will not be able to plan around. You set up an irrevocable trust to own life insurance carrying a death benefit equal to the amount of the anticipated taxes. When you die, the trust collects the insurance and uses the proceeds to pay your estate taxes. In effect, you've "pre-paid" your estate taxes through an insurance company, generally for only a small percentage of the actual liability.

ILLUSTRATION

Simone, in her mid-50s, expects to owe $300,000 in estate taxes. She establishes a trust that purchases a policy insuring her life for that amount. The policy requires annual premium payments of $9,000 per year for seven years. Simone has funded a $300,000 estate tax liability for $63,000.

Note in the illustration above that Simone used an irrevocable trust to own her insurance. If she had owned the policy herself, the death benefit would be included in her estate, and she'd owe taxes on an additional $300,000. Because the tax laws do not deem her to be the owner of assets in an irrevocable trust, Simone avoids having the death benefit counted as part of her estate.

Lesbian and gay couples who only expect to owe estate taxes on the second death might consider a special type of insurance called *survivorship life insurance* (some companies actually market this as "second-to-die insurance"). As the name implies, survivorship life does not pay a death benefit until the second of two insureds passes away, allowing for a lower premium payment. Generally, survivorship life insurance is marketed to married couples, who never need to fund an estate tax liability until the second death. Nevertheless, if your situation fits these circumstances and you can find this type of coverage, it will further lower the cost of "prepaying" your estate tax bill.

Remember that shopping for survivorship life is no different than making any other insurance purchase. All of the rules discussed earlier in the book for buying life insurance apply here as well. Work only with highly rated companies, obtain quotations from several insurance companies, carefully compare policy illustrations, and work with an agent or broker knowledgeable about both this type of policy and the special needs of lesbian and gay clients.

FEDERAL ESTATE TAX TRAPS
FOR LESBIAN AND GAY COUPLES

In addition to unique planning opportunities, lesbian and gay couples need to be aware of some possible estate tax traps that may arise because the tax law does not treat them the same as married couples.

Joint Property

When two people own property as joint tenants with rights of survivorship, they usually assume they own the property equally. In fact, if ownership is to be unequal, property generally must be held as tenants in common, not joint tenants. This is an important distinction for estate tax planning purposes, since the share of the joint property you own—or are deemed to own—will be included in your gross estate.

Thus, for lesbian and gay couples, each partner might be inclined to conclude that 50 percent of the value of joint property will be included in his or her estate. However, for unmarried joint tenants, the tax law makes a different presumption: namely, that 100 percent of the property is included in the estate of the first partner to die. Of course, 100 percent of the value of the property is included in the second partner's estate when he or she dies. The effect of this presumption is to impose estate tax on half the property an extra time. Again, there is a special exception in the law that protects married couples from this result.

It is possible to overcome this presumption, but only if you can prove to the satisfaction of the Internal Revenue Service that you and your partner each contributed equally to the purchase and upkeep of the property in question. This imposes a very high burden of proof on gay couples, requiring perhaps decades of detailed paperwork to document equal contribution over the life of the joint ownership. Often, a history of income tax returns where equal amounts were claimed as deductions for mortgage interest and property taxes can help meet this burden of proof. In addition, however, years of account statements and cancelled checks proving equal contribution for the downpayment and the cost of any improvements may be necessary to prevail.

Adding a Partner's Name to a Deed

It's not uncommon when a couple meets that one or both of them already own a house or condo. In time, they may decide to combine households. At some point, the person who owns the residence decides it would be appropriate to add his or her partner's name to the deed for the property. While this isn't necessarily a bad idea, there may be some unanticipated consequences.

First, if the owner of the house has more than $20,000 in equity, the gesture is likely to give rise to a taxable gift. By adding his or her partner's name to the deed, the owner is gifting half of his or her equity. When the value of that gift exceeds $10,000 (i.e., half of $20,000), it exceeds the gift tax annual exclusion and becomes taxable. There are ways to work around this problem, including gradual transfer of title through the use of a trust. A competent estate planner can help you with this.

Next, there are some important non-tax traps that can arise when re-titling real estate. It is likely that the owner would be in violation of the terms of the mortgage if he or she changed the deed without the lender's permission. Similarly, an owner runs the risk of voiding the title insurance he or she purchased when settling on the house unless the transfer is structured very carefully. Again, if you are contemplating the addition of a partner's name to your deed, consult with an attorney knowledgeable in both estate planning and real estate law *who understands both these issues* before you proceed.

Partners Who Pool Income

The gift tax rules create a potentially serious tax trap for lesbian and gay couples whose income is very unequal. The theory runs like this: if you and your partner pool your incomes and share expenses, one of you is making a gift to the other (unless your incomes are exactly equal). In such a case, one way to value the gift is to say that the partner with the higher income has given half of his or her "excess" income to the other partner. If that gift exceeds $10,000, it's taxable. Thus, if there is an income differential greater than $20,000 in the relationship, it is theoretically possible to conclude that one partner has made a taxable gift to the other. Once again, it should be noted that the tax law protects married couples from this problem.

One way to plan for this possibility is to keep good records documenting joint expenditures. If the "lower income" partner can demonstrate that he or she paid for his or her own living expenses, the gift theory may be harder to sustain. In such a case, the "excess" income spent by the higher income partner might be attributable to his or her personal enjoyment, making it harder to categorize the expenditures as a gift.

Keep in mind, too, that the issue is only likely to come to the IRS' attention in the context of an estate tax audit. When an estate tax return is selected for audit, the IRS agent generally reviews prior gifts (since prior gifts in excess of the gift tax annual exclusion have the effect of lowering the amount of the estate tax exemption). In conducting the audit, circumstances may come to the agent's attention causing him or her to pursue this line of reasoning. It's also worth pointing out that there are no recorded cases of the IRS taking this approach to gifts and gay couples. Nevertheless, the theory is sound, and it's an issue with enormous potential consequences both for the lesbian and gay community and for some gay couples. It may be just a matter of time before some IRS agent somewhere decides to take this position in an estate tax audit, creating a potentially nightmarish tax liability.

CHAPTER 15

State Death Taxes

When you die, the potential tax consequences are not limited to Federal law. Every state has in place its own system for taxing transfers of property at death. While the rules vary slightly from state to state, these taxes take one of two forms: an estate tax that "piggybacks" on the federal tax, or an *inheritance tax* levied on the total value of your estate. If you live in a state that piggybacks its tax onto the federal estate tax system, the planning you do to avoid the latter will also serve to avoid the former. However, for lesbians and gay men, states that impose separate inheritance taxes present a unique set of challenges.

Inheritance tax rates vary widely, but are much lower than estate tax rates. The actual rate imposed depends on the nature of the relationship between the donor and the donee; immediate family members are taxed at a lower rate, friends at a higher one. Maryland, for example, imposes a rate of 1 percent on transfers to family members, and 10 percent on transfers to other individuals. In all states that impose an inheritance tax, the higher rate applies to transfers between partners in gay relationships (because they are not legally married).

Moreover, inheritance taxes don't allow a universal $625,000 exemption like the federal estate tax does. Again, the exemption depends on the relationship: spouses usually are entitled to an unlimited exemption. Friends—including surviving partners of gay relationships—receive an exemption of between $0 and $1,000, depending on the state.

With virtually no exemption and comparatively high rates, surviving gay partners are subject to a significant potential financial burden in the

18 states that impose inheritance taxes. The table below outlines the situation state-by-state:

FIGURE 15-1
STATE INHERITANCE TAXES IMPOSED
ON DOMESTIC PARTNERS

State	Rate(s) Applicable to Partner	Exemption to Partner	Tax on $625,000 Left to Partner
Connecticut	8%–14%	$1,000	$94,500
Delaware	10%–16%	1,000	96,400
Indiana	10%–20%	100	90,000
Iowa	15%	0	89,700
Kansas	10%–15%	0	85,700
Kentucky	6%–16%	500	96,700
Louisiana	5%–10%	500	62,200
Maryland	10%	0	62,500
Montana	8%–32%	0	177,500
Nebraska	6%–18%	500	109,900
New Hampshire	18%	0	112,500
New Jersey	15%–16%	500	94,000
New York	2%–21%	108,000 (approx)	30,700
North Carolina	8%–17%	0	78,900
Ohio	2%–7%	7,000 (approx)	31,800
Oklahoma	1%–15%	0	62,900
Pennsylvania	15%	0	93,700
South Dakota	6%–30%	100	175,600

As you can see, inheritance taxes threaten to consume a disproportionate share of a gay couple's nest egg in these states.

Stephanie, a New Jersey resident, dies leaving her entire $625,000 estate to her partner Elyse. While Stephanie does not owe any Federal estate taxes, she owes New Jersey inheritance taxes of $94,000, about one-sixth of her estate.

Moreover, unlike the Federal estate tax, which is intended to target high net-worth individuals, state inheritance taxes actually can be an even greater problem for moderate income lesbian and gay couples. Consider this illustration:

Frank and Jeff are a retired couple in their late 60's living in Pennsylvania. They both receive Social Security retirement benefits. Together they own a house worth $80,000. Frank has $20,000 in savings, and Jeff has $30,000. Frank dies, leaving his entire $60,000 estate (one-half of house and savings) to Jeff. The state inheritance tax due is $9,000.

There is another implication to be drawn from these illustrations. Inheritance taxes, of course, are paid in cash, which means they must be satisfied from the liquid portion of your estate. In addition to reducing by as much as 10% to 15% the size of a surviving partner's inheritance, these taxes also threaten to consume the income-producing portion of your estate. This could leave your partner unable to maintain his or her standard of living.

In the last illustration, it's very likely that Frank and Jeff were dependent on the modest income their $50,000 in savings generated each year. $9,000, or nearly 20% of that, had to go to pay state inheritance taxes.

There are a limited number of strategies available to gay couples who face this situation. If your liquid assets are sufficient, earmarking a portion of them to satisfy the anticipated inheritance tax bill is one option. Another approach might be to adapt the life insurance planning techniques discussed in the chapter on Federal estate taxes. By purchasing extra insurance, you and your partner may be able to fund an anticipated inheritance tax liability without depleting your other assets.

Finally, note that if you own vacation or rental property in one of the eighteen "inheritance tax states," that state will impose the tax on the transfer of that property when you die—even if you live in another state at the time of your death. While this rule only applies to real estate, it will require additional planning for people affected by it.

PART VI

Life's Other Certainty:
Income Tax Planning

CHAPTER 16

Income Tax Basics

Although the nation's tax laws seem to read like hieroglyphics, requiring a legion of tax attorneys and certified public accountants to decipher, there is at some level a fundamental structure underlying how you compute your taxes each year. The sections of the Form 1040, U.S. Individual Income Tax Return, actually follow a sort of formula in reaching the end result: your tax liability. That formula looks like this:

FIGURE 16-1
FORMULA FOR COMPUTING INDIVIDUAL INCOME TAXES

Total Income

– Adjustments to Income

Adjusted Gross Income

Adusted Gross Income

– Itemized or Standard Deduction

– Personal Exemptions

Taxable Income

continues

(continued)

FORMULA FOR COMPUTING INDIVIDUAL INCOME TAXES

Tax Rate from Tax Rate Table

– Credits

+ Other Taxes
_____

Total Tax

– Payments
_____

Refund or Balance Due

_____

This chapter uses these concepts from the 1040 to explain the basics of how the income tax works, noting issues important to lesbians and gay men along the way.

Filing Status

Before diving in, a brief discussion of a concept fundamental to much of the individual income tax structure is in order: *filing status*. There are four filing statuses, driven largely by a taxpayer's familial status: single, head of household, married filing a joint return, and married filing a separate return. The passage in 1996 of the Defense of Marriage Act ensures that, at least for now, lesbian and gay couples may not use either of the married filing statuses.

Thus, unless you are in the process of ending a heterosexual marriage or can qualify for head of household status, you must use the single filing status. Because the majority of lesbians and gay men must use the single filing status, it is assumed throughout the rest of the book unless otherwise noted.

The rules for claiming head of household status can be a little tricky. It is available to single taxpayers who either: (1) pay more than half the cost of keeping up the main home of a parent they are entitled to claim as a dependent; or (2) pay over half the cost of keeping up the main home of themselves and a child, foster child, or related dependent who actually lives with them for more than half the year.

Your filing status has an impact on several components of the formula above: the amount of your standard deduction and the tax rate table you use to compute your tax liability. The standard deduction is higher and the tax rates lower for married couples filing joint returns than for single filers. Your filing status also determines your eligibility for a number of tax benefits (deductions and credits) that get "phased-out" for people with high incomes. Generally speaking, the threshold for these phase-outs is higher for joint filers than for single filers. Thus, the unavailability of the joint filing status puts lesbian and gay couples at a disadvantage compared to married straight couples.

Total Income

U.S. tax law takes the broadest possible approach to defining income. Basically, any money, property, or services you receive in exchange for your own money, property, or services is considered income, unless the law contains a specific provision excluding it. For individual taxpayers, the 1040 divides income into the following categories:

FIGURE 16-2
TYPES OF INCOME

Type	Examples
Wages, salaries, tips	W-2 income, taxable fringe benefits, unreported tips
Interest	From: checking, savings, money markets, bonds, escrow accounts
Dividends	From: stocks, mutual funds
State Tax Refunds	Refunds of amounts claimed as itemized deductions on a prior return
Alimony	Payments from an ex-spouse pursuant to a divorce settlement or property agreement
Business Income or Loss	From your sole proprietorship (Schedule C)
Capital Gain or Loss	From the sale of: stocks, bonds, or real estate (Schedule D)
Other Gains or Losses	From the sale of business property (Form 4797)
IRA Distributions	Taxable portion of IRA distributions
Pensions and Annuities	Taxable portion of employer plan and annuity payments

continues

(continued)

Type	Examples
Rental Income or Loss	From rental real estate you own (Schedule E)
Royalties	Book, music, film royalties (Schedule E)
Schedule K-1 Income or Loss	From interests you own in a partnership, S corporation, or trust (Schedule E)
Farm Income or Loss	From farm activities (Schedule F)
Unemployment Compensation	State unemployment insurance benefits
Social Security Benefits	If your income is over $25,000 (single), a portion of your Social Security benefits are taxable
Other Income	Jury duty pay, lottery winnings, gambling winnings, prize money, election worker pay, value of bartered property, hobby income

You may have noticed in the first item on the table above a reference to taxable fringe benefits. Odd as it may seem, all of the benefits your employer provides—health insurance, retirement, qualified employee discounts, and so on—are only excluded from your income because there are specific provisions in the tax law to that affect. In fact, any fringe benefit that falls outside one of these provisions *is* included in your income.

This works an unusual hardship for lesbian and gay couples who are fortunate enough to have access to *domestic partner benefits* through one or both of their employers. That's because the rules that exclude health insurance from income only apply to yourself, your legal spouse, and your dependents. Unless he or she happens to qualify as your dependent, health insurance coverage your employer provides for your partner (or your partner's employer provides for you) does not qualify for the exclusion. You and your partner are not a family as far as the tax law is concerned. Your employer will report the value of that additional coverage to you as income. The difference between the value of single coverage (which is not taxable to you) and the value of the combined coverage you and your partner receive will be included on your W-2 form at the end of the year.

ILLUSTRATION

Marcie and Karen are partners. Karen is a self-employed land-scaper. Marcie is a programmer for Cutting Edge Software. Cutting Edge offers domestic partner health insurance benefits. Because Karen would otherwise have to buy her own insurance, she and Marcie sign up for Cutting Edge's domestic partner benefits. Cutting Edge pays $270 per month to cover Marcie and Karen; individual coverage for Marcie would cost $160 per month. Cutting Edge includes the $110 per month difference between the dual coverage and the individual coverage ($270 – $160) on Marcie's W-2 at the end of the year. Marcie pays tax on an additional $1,320.

Because you will have to pay tax on any benefits your employer provides for your partner, you will need to determine whether it is more cost-effective to take advantage of domestic partner benefits or to have your partner obtain his or her own coverage.

ILLUSTRATION

Using the facts in the last illustration, assume that the difference between individual and family coverage is $280 per month (or $3,360 per year). Also assume that, in Marcie's combined Federal and state marginal tax bracket, she will pay an additional $1,344 in tax if she elects to cover Karen at work. Through the local small business league, Karen can obtain HMO coverage for $100 per month, or $1,200 per year. It would be $144 cheaper for Marcie and Karen if they did not take advantage of the domestic partner benefits available through Marcie's employer.

In addition to crunching the numbers, you and your partner should consider some non-economic factors: Do you both have employer-provided coverage? If two plans are available, how do they compare? How long will the covered partner's employment continue? Where else can the other non-covered partner obtain insurance? In the end, if the dollar difference is nominal, you may be better off choosing the option that is more likely to assure long-term access to quality health insurance coverage.

Adjusted Gross Income

The tax law singles out certain important deductions for special treatment. It calls them *adjustments to income*. Adjustments are subtracted from your total income to reach a critical number on your tax return: your *adjusted gross income (AGI)*. AGI is used to determine your eligibility for a host of tax breaks. If your AGI exceeds certain dollar amounts, which can vary with your filing status, then your itemized deductions, personal exemptions, and other tax benefits are reduced or even eliminated.

Adjustments to income include: deductions for qualifying IRA contributions; payments into special medical savings accounts; certain moving expenses not reimbursed by your employer; one-half of self-employment taxes paid, Keogh, SEP-IRA and SIMPLE retirement plan contributions; penalties for early withdrawals from CDs; and, alimony paid to a former spouse. Some of these adjustments are self-explanatory (e.g., self-employment taxes, moving expenses, alimony). The retirement-related adjustments, which can offer important tax planning opportunities for many people, are discussed in chapter 17.

Itemized or Standard Deductions

In addition to adjustments, the tax law creates another type of deduction for individual taxpayers: the personal deduction. You have two options for handling personal deductions: you can claim either a pre-set amount (called the *standard deduction*), or you can claim the actual amount of your eligible expenses (called *itemized deductions*). The amount of the standard deduction varies by filing status, and increases slightly each year for inflation. For 1998, the standard deduction for single filers is $4,250. Additional standard deduction amounts ($1,050 in 1998) are available to taxpayers over 65 and/or legally blind.

The advantage of the standard deduction is that you can automatically claim it without having to prove anything or keep any records. The advantage to itemizing is that, if your total eligible expenses are higher than your standard deduction, you can lower your tax bill. Remember, you are allowed to claim either the standard or your itemized deductions, whichever is higher.

If you do choose to itemize, you must complete Schedule A, Itemized Deductions. Note that the actual amount you can claim for several of the itemized deductions are subject to a "floor" based on your AGI. That is, you may only claim those deductions above a specified percentage of your AGI. A description of each of the itemized deduction categories follows.

1. **Medical and Dental Expenses.** You may deduct amounts spent for qualifying health-related treatments (doctors, dentists, eyeglasses, prescriptions, etc.), provided you were not reimbursed by an insurance company for the amount you are deducting. The medical and dental expense deduction is subject to a 7.5-percent floor.

   ILLUSTRATION

   Joan's AGI is $40,000. Her medical expenses are $3,001. She can deduct $1 of medical expenses on Schedule A [$3,001 – ($40,000 × 7.5%)].

   As you can see from the illustration, it is difficult to get over the 7.5-percent floor. Generally, you must have very high medical expenses, very low income, and/or no medical insurance to qualify for this deduction.

2. **Taxes You Paid.** Include in this category state and local income taxes withheld from your paycheck, as well as amounts you paid for state and local taxes for prior years. Real estate taxes and personal property taxes also fall in this category. Do not include state sales taxes, federal taxes, Social Security or Medicare taxes; they are not deductible.

   For lesbian and gay couples, each partner should include only his or her share of real estate taxes paid on jointly-owned property.

   ILLUSTRATION

   Karen and Monica own a house together. Karen pays 40 percent of the expenses and Monica pays 60 percent. Property taxes are $1,500. Karen should claim $600 ($1,500 × 40%) and Monica $900 ($1,500 × 60%) on their respective Schedule As.

3. **Interest You Paid.** Interest you pay on certain types of debt can be claimed as an itemized deduction. This includes home mortgage in-

terest, home equity loan interest, points paid to buy your primary residence, and investment interest. Most of these deductions involve debt secured by a home.

For lesbian and gay couples, each partner should report only his or her share of mortgage interest and points paid.

ILLUSTRATION

Same facts as in the last illustration. Mortgage interest paid is $10,000. Karen would deduct $4,000 ($10,000 × 40%) and Monica would deduct $6,000 ($10,000 × 60%) on their respective Schedule As.

Because lesbian and gay couples cannot file joint tax returns, there is a special reporting requirement they must satisfy with respect to jointly-owned property. Your lender reports to the IRS the mortgage interest you paid on Form 1098. The Internal Revenue Service records this information only under the first social security number listed on the 1098. The partner whose social security number is either listed second on the 1098 or not at all must attach a statement to his or her tax return providing the name and address of the other partner (i.e., the one IRS "recorded").

In addition, each partner must report his or her share of the mortgage interest deduction on different lines of the Schedule A. The partner listed first on the 1098 uses line 10, "Home mortgage interest and points reported to you on Form 1098"; the "second" partner uses line 11, "Home mortgage interest not reported to you on Form 1098." The second partner also writes "See attached" on Schedule A next to Line 11.

ILLUSTRATION

Same facts as in the last illustration. Form 1098 lists Monica's name and social security number first. Monica reports her interest on line 10 of Schedule A. Karen reports her interest on line 11. In addition, Karen also must attach the following statement to her return:

FIGURE 16-3
ATTACHMENT TO TAX RETURN FOR "SECOND" PARTNER CLAIMING MORTGAGE INTEREST DEDUCTION

SUPPLEMENTAL INFORMATION TO SCHEDULE A
LINE 11—HOME MORTGAGE INTEREST
NOT REPORTED ON FORM 1098
TAX YEAR 19XX

<u>Taxpayer</u>

Karen Taxpayer   Social Security # 123-45-6789

The following person received Form 1098 for deductible home mortgage interest on a jointly-owned property.

Monica Jones
123 Main Street
Our Town, My State 12345

4. **Gifts to Charity.** This category includes both cash and property donated to tax-deductible charities. Be sure to get a detailed receipt for all contributions of property. Although an organization may sound like a charity, contributions to political organizations, political action committees, and organizations that lobby are not deductible.

If you give or pledge to give more than $250 at any one time during the year, you must obtain a receipt from the charity in order to claim the deduction. Your cancelled check will not suffice. Separate contributions, such as $10 in the collection basket at church each week, are not subject to this rule, even if they exceed the $250 annual limit.

There is a limit on the amount of charitable deductions you may claim in one year. Generally, this limit is 50 percent of your AGI, but it drops to 30 percent or even 20 percent if you donate certain kinds of property to certain kinds of charities.

Note that you may not claim a charitable deduction for the value of your time if you do volunteer work. However, ordinary and necessary expenses you incur in the course of your volunteer work may be claimed.

Jose is a partner in a local CPA firm. His firm bills his time at $150 per hour. Jose does volunteer work at the local lesbian and gay community center preparing tax returns for low-income community members. He may not claim a charitable deduction for the value of his time spent preparing returns, but is allowed to deduct the cost of any out-of-pocket expenses (photocopies, postage, adding machine tape).

5. **Casualty and Theft Losses.** You may deduct the value of any property lost as a result of casualty or theft that is not reimbursed by insurance, but only to the extent the unreimbursed loss exceeds both $100 and 10 percent of your AGI. Because of this 10-percent floor, you are unlikely to be able to take advantage of this deduction unless your loss is uninsured and substantial—clearly not the kind of tax savings you should be hoping for!

6. **Miscellaneous Itemized Deductions.** Miscellaneous itemized deductions usually arise from expenses that generate income but that you can't claim elsewhere on your tax return. They come in two varieties: subject to a 2-percent-of-AGI floor and not subject to a 2-percent floor. The IRS publishes a list of miscellaneous itemized deductions *not* subject to the floor; if an expense is not listed, it's subject to the floor. Gambling expenses are the only common item on this very short list, and most miscellaneous itemized deductions are subject to the 2-percent floor.

   Common examples of these deductions include: (1) unreimbursed job expenses; (2) safe deposit box rental fees; (3) legal and accounting fees, if the services produced income (e.g., you sue a former employer for back wages); (4) fees paid for investment, custodial, or trust accounts (including IRAs); (5) dues paid to a union or professional association; (6) expenses paid for education (books, seminars, magazines), but only if the education is required by your employer or it produces income; (7) expenses from a hobby, but only up to the amount of any income you reported from the hobby; and, (8) tax return preparation fees.

Many taxpayers seem to operate under the assumption that deducting job-related expenses remains America's last great tax dodge. There are a number of reasons this simply isn't so. First, most people find it hard to get over the 2-percent floor. Second, the expenses have to be required by your employer or you can't deduct them. Commuting expenses are never deductible, and clothing expenses are only deductible if your clothes can't be worn anywhere other than work (e.g., a uniform). Finally, high deductions for unreimbursed business expenses often are an IRS audit flag. By all means claim the deductions you are entitled to, but otherwise try to channel your tax planning energies to more productive areas.

A final point regarding itemized deductions: if your AGI is over $124,500 (1998 amount), the total amount of the itemized deductions you may claim is reduced. The formula for computing this phase-out is pretty complicated, and it only applies to some of the itemized deductions. Although the phase-out in theory can reduce your itemized deductions by up to 80 percent, in practice most taxpayers affected by it feel a nip more on the order of 5 percent to 10 percent. Nevertheless, if your AGI is in excess of the limit, you should consult a tax advisor to see how the phase-out affects you.

Personal Exemptions

It's hard to get real technical in explaining the personal exemption deduction. Basically, it's an amount the tax law allows you to subtract from income just for being alive that year. You are allowed to claim one personal exemption for yourself, one for your spouse, and one for each dependent. For 1998, each exemption is worth $2,700.

Like itemized deductions, the amount of your personal exemption deduction starts getting phased-out once your AGI exceeds certain amounts. For single filers, the phase-out begins at $124,500 in 1998. This phase-out can go all the way down to $0, and it does happen to taxpayers whose AGI is more than $125,000 above the limit.

The test for determining whether someone is a dependent for purposes of claiming a personal exemption deduction is not the same as the test used to determine whether someone is a dependent for purposes of claiming the head of household filing status. To be a dependent for personal exemption purposes, the person you are claiming must meet *all* of the following:

(1) he or she must either be a relative or live with you for the entire year; (2) unless he or she is your child, his or her total income must be less than the amount of the personal exemption deduction; (3) unless you and an ex-spouse agree otherwise, he or she must receive at least 50 percent of his or her total support for the year from you; (4) if he or she has a spouse, they cannot file a joint tax return; and, (5) he or she must be either a U.S. citizen or a resident of the United States, Canada, or Mexico.

Claiming a Partner as a Dependent. In gay relationships, one partner may occasionally seek to claim the other as a dependent. In order to accomplish this, however, the "dependent" partner must meet all five of the criteria listed above. Most partners exceed the modest income limit included in the test, causing a loss of the exemption. In addition, the exemption is not allowed where the relationship between the taxpayer and the dependent violates local law; IRS has given reason to believe this may be an issue for gay couples in states where sodomy statutes remain on the books.

Note, too, that there are tax consequences to your partner if you claim him or her as a dependent. Your partner cannot claim a personal exemption deduction on his or her own tax return. Also, if your partner uses the standard deduction, it will be limited to the greater of his or her actual wages or $700 (in 1998).

In limited circumstances, it can be advantageous to claim a partner as a dependent. This often arises when only one partner has income, and often a high income in search of some offsetting deductions; perhaps the other partner is ill, or in school, or even between jobs. Also, if your partner has very high medical expenses and qualifies as your dependent, you can claim as an itemized deduction any of those expenses you actually pay (subject to the 7.5-percent floor). This can be a help to couples facing high medical bills as a result of HIV or other serious illness.

TAX RATES

Many of the strategies used to reduce taxes require you to understand your marginal tax bracket, as well as the difference between marginal and effective tax rates. The federal income tax system uses a progressive rate structure. The current tax brackets are 15 percent, 28 percent, 31 percent, 36 percent, and 39.6 percent. Brackets increase at different income levels for each filing status, and the levels are adjusted each year for inflation. The 1998 tax rates for single filers are:

FIGURE 16-4
1998 TAX RATE TABLE FOR SINGLE FILERS

If taxable income is	then the tax is
Under $25,350	15% of the amount
$25,350–$61,400	$3,802.50, plus 28% of the amount above $25,350
$61,401–$128,100	$13,896.50, plus 31% of the amount above $61,400
$128,101–$278,450	$34,573.50, plus 36% of the amount above $128,100
Above $278,450	$88,699.50, plus 39.6% of the amount above $278,450

An important feature of this progressive rate structure is that different segments of a person's income are subject to tax at different rates.

ILLUSTRATION

Your taxable income is $75,000. The first $25,350 of that amount is taxed at 15 percent, the portion between $25,350 and $61,400 is taxed at 28 percent, and the rest is taxed at 31 percent.

Your *marginal tax rate* is the rate you pay on your last dollar of taxable income (i.e., the dollar "at the margin").

ILLUSTRATION

In the last illustration, your marginal tax rate is 31 percent.

Knowing your marginal tax rate allows you to determine how much you will lower your taxes if you adopt a given tax planning strategy.

ILLUSTRATION

You are considering a year-end charitable contribution of $1,000. Because money is tight around the holidays, however, you want to understand how much you'll save in taxes by making the contribution. You need to know your marginal tax rate to do this. If you're in the 15 percent bracket, for example, your savings will be $150 ($1,000 × 15%). If you're in the 31 percent bracket, the savings increase to $310 ($1,000 × 31%).

While your marginal tax rate can help you evaluate specific tax planning strategies, you can use your *effective tax rate* to measure your overall tax burden.

ILLUSTRATION

Your total income for the year is $50,000, and you paid $8,000 in taxes. Your effective tax rate is 16 percent ($8,000/$50,000). (By contrast, your marginal tax rate is 28 percent.)

When computing marginal tax rates, you should consider state as well as federal income taxes. This provides you with a more accurate way to measure the impact of tax planning strategies (using your combined marginal rates) as well as your overall tax burden (using your combined effective rates).

ILLUSTRATION

Same facts as the last illustration. You live in Illinois, which has a flat 3 percent income tax. You pay $1,500 in Illinois state tax for the year. Your combined marginal tax rate is 31 percent (28% + 3%). Your combined effective tax rate is 19 percent ($\frac{\$8,000+\$1,500}{\$50,000}$).

Note that marginal rates are determined with reference to taxable income, whereas effective rates are determined with reference to total income.

CREDITS

It's very helpful in tax planning to distinguish a tax deduction from a tax credit: a deduction is used to offset income, while a credit is used to offset the taxes you pay. Thus, credits are more valuable than deductions.

ILLUSTRATION

You are in the 31 percent marginal tax bracket. A $1,000 deduction will enable you to reduce your tax bill by $310. By contrast, a $1,000 credit will enable you to reduce your tax bill by $1,000.

Important credits for many taxpayers are: the new tax credit for children under 17; the earned income tax credit for low-income workers; the credit for foreign taxes paid; the credit for child and dependent care expenses paid; and, the credit for the elderly and disabled.

OTHER TAXES

In addition to the regular income tax, there are several other taxes you may encounter when preparing your return. When you sell certain assets, such as stock or real estate, you pay capital gains tax—and not income tax—on the gain you realize. Congress has expanded the preferential treatment the tax law affords capital gains, giving rise to many important planning opportunities.

If you are self-employed, you must pay both the employer's and the employee's share of Social Security and Medicare taxes. These are known as self-employment taxes.

If you have very high income and numerous deductions, you may be subject to what is known as the alternative minimum tax (AMT). As the name suggests, the purpose of the AMT is to ensure that everyone pays at least some income tax. In order to achieve this goal, however, Congress created a very complex regime. Few taxpayers are actually affected by the AMT, although some predict the number will grow in future years. Right now, most of those who must suffer through it are either very high earners or individuals with a large one-time jump in income.

If you hire domestic employees (housekeepers, gardeners, drivers), you must report and pay on your 1040 their social security taxes, federal unemployment taxes, and any federal income taxes they ask you to withhold.

A variety of penalty taxes can be imposed if you mishandle your retirement savings. These are covered in chapter 18.

Now that you understand the mechanics of how the individual income tax system works, review the next two chapters to explore ways to use those mechanics to lower your tax bill.

CHAPTER 17

Tax-Smart Investing

Because the writers of the nation's tax laws want to encourage saving and investing, there are a number of important investment-related tax planning strategies. The law contains incentives that allow you to do one or more of the following: (1) exclude from income the investments you make (e.g., 401(k)s, deductible IRAs); (2) defer payment of taxes on your investment earnings to some future time (e.g., 401(k)s, all IRAs, annuities); and/or, (3) take advantage of reduced or eliminated tax rates (e.g., municipal bonds, capital gains). The strategies that result from these rules can have an influence on both how you invest and what you choose to invest in.

INDIVIDUAL RETIREMENT ACCOUNTS

Thanks to 1997's big tax bill, *individual retirement accounts* (IRAs) now come in three major varieties: deductible IRAs, non-deductible IRAs, and Roth IRAs. IRAs offer important tax and retirement planning opportunities. In order to know which IRA option makes the most sense for you, you must understand the rules applicable to each.

> *Deductible IRAs.* You may contribute the lesser of your earned income or $2,000 to an IRA each year. The contribution is fully deductible on your income tax return unless you are covered both by a retirement plan at work and your AGI is over $30,000 (1998 figure for single filers). The amount of your deduction gets reduced as your AGI exceeds this limit, until your contribution becomes

non-deductible at $40,000 (i.e., the phase-out range is $10,000). Because of changes in the law, this range will increase slowly over the next several years, until it reaches $50,000 to $60,000 in 2005. You can tell if you are covered by an employer's plan by looking at your Form W-2; if either the "Pension Plan" or the "Deferred Compensation" squares in Box 15 are checked, then you are covered, and your AGI must be below the limit to claim the deduction. If you are not covered by an employer's plan, you are eligible to make a deductible IRA contribution regardless of your AGI. Earnings from an IRA grow tax-free; instead, taxes are paid when withdrawals are made from the account. A complex set of rules governs IRA withdrawals, including penalties for withdrawing funds too soon, or leaving them in an account too long. The rules regarding IRA withdrawals are discussed in the next chapter.

Non-deductible IRAs. Non-deductible IRAs function in all respects like deductible IRAs except, of course, in your ability to claim a deduction for the initial contribution on your income tax return. There are no AGI or other limits on your ability to make non-deductible IRA contributions.

Roth IRAs. The '97 tax law created a new Roth IRA with some unique advantages. No current deduction is allowed for contributions; however, as long as funds are left in the account for the longer of five years or until you reach age $59\frac{1}{2}$, withdrawals are completely free of tax. Penalties apply if you violate these rules; there are exceptions to the penalties in the case of certain hardships. Again, the withdrawal rules for IRAs are discussed in the next chapter.

Which IRA is Right for You?

Once you have established which type(s) of IRA you are eligible to use in a given year, how do you know which one is the best to choose? In order to answer this question it may be helpful to establish what patterns your choices are likely to follow:

1. If you are eligible for a deductible IRA (either because you are not covered by an employer's plan or because you are covered by an employer's plan but are below the AGI limit), you also will be

eligible for a non-deductible IRA and a Roth IRA; you can choose from all three options.

2. Even if you are not eligible for a deductible IRA (because you are both covered by an employer's plan and above the AGI limit), you may still be eligible to choose between a Roth IRA or a non-deductible IRA; if your AGI is below the Roth IRA limits, you can choose between the last two options.

3. Even if you are not eligible for either a deductible IRA (because you are both covered by an employer's plan and above the AGI limit) or a Roth IRA (because you are above the AGI limit) you are always eligible for a non-deductible IRA.

Since your total contributions to all types of IRAs is limited to a combined $2,000 per year, it's important to choose your IRA carefully. Consider the following with respect to each of the three patterns above:

In the first pattern, the non-deductible IRA cannot really compete with the superior tax advantages of the other two options, so for all practical purposes your choice is between a deductible IRA and a Roth IRA. In essence, you are trying to compare the value of the current tax deduction (for deductible IRAs) to the value of the future income exclusion (for Roth IRAs). Although the lure of a current deduction is always tempting, the future exclusion in this case is likely to be of greater value. In other words, the tax savings from Roth IRAs in your retirement years are likely to be more valuable than the tax savings from an IRA deduction this year. An additional consideration: under current law, withdrawals from regular IRAs are included in your AGI, increasing the likelihood that your Social Security benefits will be subject to taxation; this isn't the case with Roth IRAs. Note, too, that Roth IRAs also avoid the minimum required distribution rules that apply to regular IRAs. Certainly, if you're already contributing to a tax-deferred account (e.g., 401(k)) at work, the Roth IRA is the better choice; it's likely to be in most other instances, as well.

In the second pattern, the Roth IRA again offers more tax advantages than the non-deductible IRA does. Assuming you qualify for Roth IRA contributions, it provides the better tax planning opportunity.

The third pattern begs the question: do non-deductible IRAs ever make sense? Bear in mind that if it is all you are eligible for and your income is very high, you probably need whatever tax breaks you can get. However, nondeductible IRAs come with all the same withdrawal restrictions as any other IRA. It is possible to replicate the non-deductible IRA's tax advantages through other investments (municipal bonds, annuities growth assets in which tax is deferred until you decide to sell the asset). Thus, while it's hard to say non-deductible IRAs are a *bad* idea, there are less restrictive alternatives.

ANNUITIES

Annuities are life insurance products that allow you to invest on a tax-advantaged basis. Because of the special tax rules that govern the treatment of money you invest through insurance products, you can defer paying tax on the earnings of an annuity policy—interest, dividends, and capital gains—until you begin receiving annuity payments. This can provide significant tax savings for investors in high marginal brackets.

Most annuities (at least those used as investment vehicles) work like this: you make monthly or quarterly payments to the annuity over a number of years. Investment decisions are made either by the issuer of the policy (fixed-rate annuities) or by the investor (variable-rate annuities); generally, only the latter are appropriate for tax-advantaged investing. After many years of tax-deferred accumulation, you begin withdrawing funds from the annuity over a specified time frame (your life, the joint lives of yourself and your partner, or a fixed number of years). It is only when the withdrawals begin that taxes are due.

There are some important things to consider before investing in annuities, however. First, you must be in a financial position to commit to regular monthly investments for a long period of time. With most annuities, you cannot miss a payment, and there are surrender charges if you abandon the annuity in the first five to seven years. Next, the insurance company offering the annuity should provide suitable investments from which to choose. You usually are restricted to a limited number of investment choices, and the performance may be less than you could obtain elsewhere. Third, the insurance company is in the annuity business to make money, so their fees are going to have an impact on your investment performance. As with any investment fee, the overall return had better justify the expense, or there is no point in incurring it. Finally, as with life insurance, you need to be certain the company you're dealing with is highly rated by the rating companies mentioned in chapter 10.

Because of these many considerations, annuities probably are appropriate only for mature investors, and not for those just starting out.

MUNICIPAL BONDS

The interest income generated by municipal bonds is exempt from federal income tax. Moreover, in most states, municipal bonds issued within the state are free of state and local taxes as well. For people who meet their current income needs from interest on their invested assets, this can mean substantial tax savings.

ILLUSTRATION

You have $100,000 to invest for meeting your current income needs. You are considering a corporate bond that earns 9 percent or a municipal bond (issued within your state) that pays 7.5 percent. While the corporate bond seems like a better deal at first glance, a closer look at the after-tax numbers shows this may not be so. The municipal bond will pay you $7,500 in interest, but it's completely tax-free. With the corporate bond, in just the 15-percent bracket, you would pay $1,350 in federal tax on your $9,000 interest income, leaving you with a net return of $7,650—*before* state income taxes. If you live in a state with just a 2 percent income tax rate (most are higher), the municipal bond provides a better after-tax return.

Of course, most bond investors are not in the 15-percent bracket; as your marginal tax bracket increases, the advantages of municipal bonds are even more compelling.

ILLUSTRATION

Use the facts from the last illustration, but assume you are in the 28-percent bracket. The municipal bond still earns $7,500, but the corporate bond now costs $2,520 in federal tax, leaving you with a return of $6,480—again, *before* state income taxes.

The states, counties, cities, and towns that issue municipal bonds know you're saving taxes on them, so they offer lower interest rates than taxable bonds. (Note the 9-percent versus 7.5-percent differential in the last two illustrations.) Nevertheless, even with the lower pre-tax return, high-quality "munis" offer a compelling case when investing for current income.

U.S. TREASURY SECURITIES

State and local governments cannot tax interest paid by the U.S. Treasury. This creates a modest tax advantage for Treasury investments, particularly if you live in a high-tax state. Combined with the unmatched security offered by the "full faith and credit" of the U.S. government (which backs every Treasury security), the state tax savings makes them very attractive to investors with a low risk tolerance and current income needs. Of course, you must still pay federal income tax on the income from these investments, limiting their utility as a tax-advantaged investment.

U.S. SAVINGS BONDS

With most bonds, you are required to pay tax on the interest income as it is earned. However, with Series EE U.S. Savings Bonds, you have the option of deferring payment of federal tax until you either redeem the bonds or they mature. Although this is an attractive option, EE Bonds generally offer comparatively low rates of return. If you are investing for medium- or long-term goals, EE Bonds may be an appropriate vehicle for the portion of your portfolio allocated to cash equivalent investments.

Other considerations with EE Bonds: In certain circumstances, parents can redeem them free of tax in order to pay for a child's college tuition. Also, like all other U.S. government securities, EE Bonds are exempt from state and local income tax.

CAPITAL GAINS

When you sell certain types of assets (stocks, bonds, real estate)—called *capital assets*—you must report on your tax return the difference between what you paid for them (your *basis*) and what you sold them for. If the sales price is higher than your basis, you must pay tax on the *capital gain*; if it is lower, within limits you can deduct the *capital loss*. 1997's big tax bill contained major changes in how capital gains are taxed. While most of the changes will benefit taxpayers, they add a tremendous level of complexity in this area of the law. You need to be familiar with these complex new rules in order to ensure that your investment decisions don't have unintended tax consequences.

The rate of capital gains tax varies based on several factors; the most important of these is how long you owned the asset before you sold it—called your *holding period*. Other considerations include the type of asset, when it is purchased, and your marginal income tax bracket. In order to keep the explanation that follows simple, the capital gains rates used in this chapter assume that your marginal bracket is above 15 percent; if you *are* in the 15-percent income tax bracket, your capital gains rate will be even lower.

If you own an asset for less than 12 months, it is a *short-term* asset, and the gain on it is taxed at the same rate as your ordinary income. There are no tax planning opportunities with short-term capital gains.

The new law created a new holding period, and it appears that financial planners and tax professionals are referring to it as *mid-term* gain; it applies to assets held more than 12 but less than 18 months. The capital gains rate on mid-term assets generally is 28 percent. If your marginal income tax bracket is 31 percent, 36 percent, or 39.6 percent, you have a modest incentive to favor investments that produce mid-term capital gains (e.g., growth mutual funds) over those that generate ordinary income (e.g., income mutual funds).

Assets owned more than 18 months receive *long-term* capital gains treatment—a rate of 20 percent, dropping to 18 percent for assets you purchase after 2000. There are several planning opportunities that arise as a result of this change. Note that most of these strategies apply to assets held outside of tax-deferral vehicles like IRAs, 401(k)s, and annuities.

First, the tax law now provides significant incentive for re-considering your investment strategy. Unless you are investing for current income needs, the tax law places a huge premium on investments that generate capital gains instead of ordinary income. Assets that produce interest or dividend income (e.g., taxable bonds, taxable bond funds, and high-yield dividend stocks) fall in the latter category. The case is compelling for those in the 31 percent, 36 percent or 39.6 percent marginal brackets.

Next, for high-bracket investors with medium- or long-term goals, the new long-term capital gains rates mean that some tax-deferred investment vehicles (annuities, variable life insurance, non-deductible IRAs) have lost a little of their luster. There are several reasons for this: (1) All withdrawals, including those attributable to capital gains, from tax-deferred investments are taxed at ordinary income rates, not the now-substantially-lower capital gains rates. (2) Generally, you can choose when to sell an asset and recognize the capital gain; combined with the new lower rates, this allows you to approximate the tax advantages available through tax-deferred investment vehicles. (3) These two considerations place a higher premium on the many restrictions that come with tax-deferred investing (e.g., waiting for $59\frac{1}{2}$ to make withdrawals). Of course, if your tax-deferred investment included a deduction for the original contribution (as with 401(k)s and deductible IRAs), then the tax benefits generally still work in your favor, regardless of your bracket.

Further, the new capital gains rules will require mutual fund managers to place increased emphasis on tax-managing their fund portfolios. Publications that rate fund performance will focus on how well funds manage their investments to take advantage of the new capital gains rules and minimize the tax exposure of their investors.

Finally, for those who are old hands at incorporating capital gains planning into their investment planning, it's important to note that the 18-month holding period for long-term gains represents a change made by the new tax law; previously, the holding period for long-term gains was only 12 months. Be sure you hold your assets long enough to take advantage of the new long-term rates.

In addition to all of the new planning opportunities that arise from the new capital gains rules, you should be aware of some benefits that can come through the strategic timing of capital losses. The way capital gains rules work, you essentially net the gains and losses from all your sales, and report the result on the front of your return.

There are two situations in which deliberately generating capital losses can be used for advantageous tax planning: (1) The law allows you to deduct up to $3,000 in *net capital losses* each year (i.e., losses in excess of your gains); you can use these losses to offset other sources of income on your return. If your net losses are more than $3,000, you can use the excess to offset income on future returns. (2) If you've had substantial short- or mid-term gains, where the rates aren't quite as favorable as for long-term gains, it may make sense to sell assets you know will generate an offsetting capital loss.

In either case, this strategy requires a careful review of your portfolio (usually at year-end) to determine whether you have non-performing assets that can appropriately be sold. Always make sure your decision is a sound one from the perspective of your investment planning; if you believe an asset's performance is likely to improve, or if a sale would be inconsistent with your buy-and-hold strategy, by all means hold onto the asset. While tax considerations are important, you should not allow them to obscure your view of the bigger picture.

CHAPTER 18

Other Tax Planning Strategies

The ability to adopt planning strategies to minimize income tax varies greatly with individual circumstances. Do you rent or own your home? Are you an employee or self-employed? What is your family (or alternative family) structure? Do you have access to tax-favored investment vehicles? Nevertheless, there are some basic planing strategies that have widespread applicability. The purpose of this chapter is to explore those strategies.

SHIFTING INCOME TO PARTNERS OR OTHER FAMILY MEMBERS

One way to lower your tax bill is to shift ownership of income-producing assets to a loved one who is in a lower tax bracket. For years, parents did this with their minor children, but several years ago Congress enacted a complex set of rules known as the *Kiddie Tax*. The Kiddie Tax, which essentially taxes a portion of a child's investment income at the parent's marginal rate, limits the utility of this particular application of income-shifting, but other attractive possibilities remain.

For lesbian and gay couples, shifting income to a partner in a lower tax bracket can be a good planning strategy, provided that doing so doesn't bump the "lower-bracket" partner into a higher bracket.

ILLUSTRATION

Carlo, who is in the 31-percent tax bracket, received $5,000 in dividend income during the past year. His partner, Andy, is in the 15-percent tax bracket. By shifting 50 percent of the stock to Andy, Carlo could reduce his tax bite by $775 ($2,500 × 31%). Andy's tax bill would go up $375 ($2,500 × 15%), for a net tax savings to the couple of $400.

There are a few cautions that come with this strategy, however. First, the higher income partner must make a bona fide transfer of assets to the lower income partner. Second, in the process of making the transfer, the couple must be careful not to run afoul of the gift tax rules, discussed in chapter 14.

ILLUSTRATION

In the last illustration, Carlo would have been required to file a gift tax return if the value of the stock he transferred to Andy was more than $10,000.

You should consider carefully both the economic and non-economic implications of transferring ownership of assets to a partner (or anyone else) before using this strategy.

If you own your own business, there may be additional ways to shift income to your partner. Again, you both have to be in different marginal tax brackets for this strategy to work. Also, there needs to be a bona fide employment relationship in which the employee-partner performs legitimate work-related tasks for the employer-partner's business.

ILLUSTRATION

Neil is a successful self-employed consultant. He is in the 39.6-percent tax bracket. His partner Stefan works part-time and is in the 15-percent tax bracket. Neil hires Stefan as a part-time office assistant, and pays him $10,000 per year. Since this is a business deduction for Neil, he saves $3,960 in income tax ($10,000 × 39.6%). On the other hand, Stefan's income tax goes up $1,500 ($10,000 × 15%), for a net savings to the couple of $2,460.

Several other factors must be considered before the final tax savings can be known. In this illustration, Neil would be obligated for (deductible) payroll taxes, unemployment taxes, and workers compensation insurance for Stefan. On the other hand, planning opportunities may arise which allow Neil to provide Stefan with tax-deductible fringe benefits (health insurance, disability insurance, retirement plans).

ILLUSTRATION

Same facts as in the last illustration. Neil contributes $2,000 to Stefan's retirement plan and pays $1,800 for his health insurance coverage. Neil's income tax is reduced by $1,505 ($3,800 × 39.6%). The net cost to Neil of providing health insurance and retirement savings to his partner through his business is $2,295 ($3,800 − $1,505).

Note, too, that neither of the last two illustrations took into consideration Neil's potential self-employment tax or state income tax savings from this strategy. If you think you or your partner can benefit from this type of tax planning, you should consult with an accountant or tax advisor to implement it properly.

TIMING OF INCOME AND EXPENSES

As an individual taxpayer, you report income and deductions on what is called the *cash basis*. In other words, you report income in the year you receive it (or have the right to receive it) and claim deductions in the year the expenses are paid. For taxpayers in a high marginal tax bracket, timing the receipt of income and expenses between tax years can be an effective strategy.

ILLUSTRATION

In December 19X1 Carlo receives a large one-time bonus from his employer. He also cashes in some EE savings bonds with accumulated interest of $10,000. The combination of the bonus and bond interest pushed him into the 39.6-percent tax bracket for the year. If he had waited until January 2 of 19X2 to cash in the bonds, when he would be back in the 31-percent tax bracket, he could have saved $860 in taxes [$10,000 × (39.6% − 31%)].

Same facts as the last illustration. Carlo decides to clean out his closets with the intention of making an end-of-year donation to charity. The thrift shop value of his donation is $3,000. Carlo neglects to drop off his donation until January 2, 19X2. Because his marginal tax rate changes, the value of the charitable deduction he will claim in 19X2 is $258 less than it would have been in 19X1 [$3,000 × (39.6% − 31%)].

As you contemplate how to apply this planning strategy to your own circumstances, remember that it also can work where the marginal bracket in 19X1 is *lower* than the anticipated bracket in 19X2—only the goal would be to shift income to the first year and expenses to the second.

You should be as strategic as possible in timing your deductions. For example, people frequently make charitable contributions just before the end of the year. While this is a good planning strategy, you also should consider whether your tax bracket is likely to be higher the following year, and if so by how much. Although a deduction now generally is worth more than a deduction a year from now, a deduction in the 15-percent bracket now is worth less than a deduction in the 28-percent bracket a year from now.

There's one other way to use timing as a tax planning strategy; it applies when the total amount of your deductions routinely puts you on the border between itemizing and claiming the standard deduction. This strategy will only work for people whose deductions hover around the standard deduction threshold each year ($4,250 for singles in 1998). For taxpayers in this range, here's one illustration of how the strategy can work:

ILLUSTRATION

Carrie is a single taxpayer who earns $35,000, making her marginal tax rate 28 percent. She does not own a home. Her employer withholds $2,400 in state income taxes each year, and she makes annual charitable contributions of $2,000. Her total deductions are $4,400, and she would qualify to itemize. However, she is only $150 over the standard deduction amount, so her additional tax savings from itemizing is only $42 ($150 ×

28%). Carrie could increase her tax savings if she contributes $3,000 to charity in 19X1, and only $1,000 in 19X2. Here's how: the extra contribution in 19X1 yields an additional $1,000 in itemized deductions, for an additional tax savings of $280 ($1,000 × 28%). In 19X2, she no longer has enough deductions to itemize, so she claims the standard deduction. Carrie lost $42 in tax savings by not itemizing in 19X2, but came out $238 ($280 – $42) ahead over the two-year period.

In order to know if this strategy can work for you, you may need to spend some time with a calculator. Remember that you can't control the timing of some deductions (e.g., payroll deductions for state income taxes), and that you can only control others to a certain degree (e.g., in the last illustration, Carrie probably could not have afforded to make all $4,000 in contributions in 19X1).

One other wrinkle to watch for with this strategy: state income taxes. Usually, if you itemize deductions on your Federal return, you also must do so on your state return (and vice-versa if you claim the standard deduction). In addition, state income tax withholdings—the largest itemized deduction for most people who use this strategy—can't be deducted on your state tax return. The net result: if you live in a high-tax state, it's possible this strategy will cost you more in state taxes than you save in Federal taxes.

TAX PLANNING WITH MULTIPLE RESIDENCES

The tax law provides an interesting planning opportunity for lesbian and gay couples who, in addition to their primary residence, wish to own more than one vacation home. The tax law allows a deduction for mortgage interest on a main home and one second home. However, because these rules apply to each partner in a gay relationship separately, gay couples who can deduct the interest on three (or even four) houses—one (or two) more than married couples can. Note, too, that "residence" has a broad definition under the tax law; as long as a structure has sleeping, cooking, and bathroom facilities, it qualifies.

ILLUSTRATION

You and your partner co-own a condo in the city. You also have a cabin at the lake for weekend getaways. You have started to think about buying a sailboat to keep at the lake. If you purchase the sailboat, you can structure the mortgage deductions like this: you each deduct half of the condo interest, one of you deducts the cabin interest, and the other deducts the sailboat interest (assuming it has a galley and a head).

In order for this arrangement to survive an IRS audit, the underlying economics have to follow the tax treatment. That is, the one of you who deducted the boat would have to make payments on it, and the one who deducted the cabin would have to make the payments on the cabin.

RENTAL REAL ESTATE

Rental real estate offers one of the few remaining opportunities for generating paper losses that can be used to offset other sources of income and reduce taxes. However, there is a very high risk factor associated with this strategy; it can be costly and time-consuming to: find good tenants, collect rent, make repairs, carry a vacant property, and abide fluctuations in the value of your property.

Here's the reward for all this risk: you can deduct up to $25,000 in excess rental real estate losses (i.e., losses in excess of your rental income). Several technical requirements must be met, but generally if you directly own and manage the property in question you'll qualify. The deduction phases out as your AGI goes above $100,000, and reaches zero at $150,000. If your income exceeds $150,000, this strategy won't work for you and a vacation home may be a better deal.

Consider the following illustration of how the deduction can work:

ILLUSTRATION

You rent out a condo for $1,000 per month, or $12,000 per year. The mortgage interest is $7,200 per year, the condo fees $2,400, property taxes $1,800, and the depreciation deduction $2,600, for a total annual deduction of $14,000. Assuming that your income is under $100,000, the $2,000 loss can be used to offset your other income. If you are in the 31-percent bracket, this will reduce your taxes by $620.

It can be difficult to find a real estate investment that will generate tax losses without also generating real out-of-pocket losses. The key is to consider the value of the depreciation deduction in determining whether a loss is a real loss or just a tax loss. Each year you can claim a depreciation deduction equal to about 3.6 percent of what you've invested in a property (less the value of the land, which cannot be depreciated).

ILLUSTRATION

In the illustration above, the $2,600 you claimed for depreciation is not a cash loss. It is, however, a tax deduction. Moreover, since your actual cash expenses only totaled $11,400, you earned $600 above what you spent on the property. The final result: a $620 tax savings and $600 in "tax-free" income!

Of course, things don't always turn out as planned. In the last illustration, what if the property sat vacant for a couple of months? Or if your tenant didn't pay the rent? Or if major repairs were required? Expenses associated with real estate are not always predictable, and cash flow can fluctuate considerably each year.

Moreover, note that the depreciation deduction comes with a kicker: when you sell the property, you must increase your gain by the total depreciation you've claimed on the property over the years.

In the end, it's safe to say that rental real estate is not a tax planning strategy suited to everybody; there are many risks involved in real estate ownership, and many strings attached to the tax deduction. Nevertheless, if the strategy has appeal, or if you unexpectedly find yourself in the landlord business (i.e., a job- or relationship-related move combined with an old residence you can't or won't sell), be sure to carefully project how the money will flow, and set aside a reserve for the unknown!

WITHDRAWALS AND DISTRIBUTIONS
FROM RETIREMENT PLANS

The tax benefits of retirement plans come with strings attached: there can be (sometimes severe) adverse tax consequences if you mishandle your "pre-tax" savings. In order to avoid these consequences, and to take advantage of some planning opportunities they present, you first need to understand four general rules:

1. If you withdraw pre-tax savings before age $59\frac{1}{2}$, you pay a 10 percent tax on the withdrawal, unless it is due to death, disability, a qualifying first-time home purchase, qualifying college expenses, leaving a job after age 55, or an "annuitized" distribution (more on this last exception below).

ILLUSTRATION

At age 35, Ilse withdraws $10,000 from her IRA to purchase a new car. She is in the 28-percent bracket. She owes $2,800 in federal income tax plus $1,000 in penalty tax, leaving her with a net of $6,200—without taking state income taxes into account. By doing this, Ilse has realized about 60 cents on the dollar from her withdrawal.

2. If you don't begin making required minimum distributions from a retirement plan (important exception: Roth IRAs) before April 1st of the year after you turn $70\frac{1}{2}$, the law imposes a 50 percent penalty on the amount you should have withdrawn.

ILLUSTRATION

You were born on May 1, 1927. You have $90,000 in an IRA account. You turned $70\frac{1}{2}$ on November 1, 1997, and therefore must begin to make withdrawals from your IRA by April 1, 1998. IRS tables say your life expectancy is 15 years, so your first withdrawal must be at least $6,000 ($90,000/15). You must continue to make minimum withdrawals every year thereafter, although you may re-compute the amount annually as IRS updates its life expectancy tables. If you were to withdraw only $5,000 in 1998, you would owe a penalty tax of $500—50 percent of the additional $1,000 you were required to withdraw.

3. If you receive a lump-sum distribution from an employer's plan (but not from an IRA), your employer must withhold 20 percent of the distribution for the payment of income taxes; there is no withholding if you arrange for a direct transfer to another plan (a new employer's plan or an IRA).

ILLUSTRATION

On June 1, 19X1, you change jobs; you have a $50,000 balance in your old employer's 401(k) plan. You decide to move the funds into an IRA account, and ask your employer to send you a check. The check arrives in the amount of $40,000 ($50,000 – 20%). If you only deposit the $40,000 into an IRA, you will owe income tax (and penalty tax if you are under $59\frac{1}{2}$) on the $10,000 your employer was required to withhold. To avoid this, you must take $10,000 from your own savings and deposit it into your new IRA within 60 days. You can claim a credit on your 19X1 tax return for the $10,000 withheld by your old employer.

ILLUSTRATION

Same facts as the previous illustration, but instead of asking your old employer to send you the 401(k) funds, you open an IRA account shortly after you change jobs, and authorize your old employer to deposit the funds into your new account. Your old employer does this. You have rolled over your retirement plan balance without any adverse tax consequences.

4. Even in retirement, the advantages of deferring tax on the earnings from retirement accounts continue to apply, and you generally should leave assets in tax-favored vehicles as long as possible.

Planning When Leaving a Job

When you leave a job—regardless of the reason—figuring out what to do with funds in an employer's retirement plan requires several important decisions. Your approach to these decisions will depend on whether you are at or near retirement.

If you are not near retirement, your goal should be to preserve the tax-favored status of the assets while continuing to obtain the best possible investment returns. First, find out whether your employer's plan *requires* you to move the funds. If it does, you will have to arrange for a direct transfer of the account balance(s) to another plan (a new employer's plan or a rollover IRA); *never* accept direct receipt of the funds yourself. If you have the option of keeping your assets in your old employer's plan, you'll need to evaluate the selections and performance of the investments available through the plan. If they are good, you should consider keeping the assets in the old plan; if you can do better elsewhere, you should transfer them (again, *directly* to a new employer's plan or a rollover IRA).

If you are at or near retirement, you face one additional choice. The basic premise regarding the advantages of tax deferral continues to apply, and it's likely that you should follow the rollover rules discussed above. However, a few additional considerations come into play:

1. If you are 55 or over and take a total withdrawal from an employer's plan before 2000, there are special *lump-sum averaging* rules that can lower the taxes you pay. Although you pay all tax in the year you receive the lump-sum, you compute that tax as if you were paying it over five years, in essence taking advantage of the 15-percent tax bracket 5 times.

2. If you are 55 or over and receive a lump-sum distribution because your employment has terminated, you would owe income tax but not the 10-percent penalty tax if you chose not to rollover the distribution.

In limited circumstances, it turns out that these modest tax breaks provide enough of a savings that it makes more sense to pay tax on retirement assets than to continue deferring it. Using any of these planning opportunities likely makes sense only if you expect to have short-term needs for the money; if you will be able to leave all or most of it untouched for several years after a pending distribution, you should roll the balance over into another tax-advantaged account.

The stakes are high when it comes to handling retirement plan distributions, so you should always consider calling in the pros if you're unsure how to proceed.

At retirement, your employer may also offer the option of converting the assets in your plan into an annuity. You usually can elect to receive payments over your life, over two joint lives, or for a fixed number of years. Unless you are very bad with money or very concerned about outliving your assets, you're generally better off taking a lump-sum and, using the same decision-making process outlined above, making distributions on your own schedule. If you want an annuity and are in a relationship, be certain the joint life option is available for yourself and your partner through your employer's plan; if it isn't, you definitely should use one of the other options outlined above.

Planning with IRAs

Generally speaking, the strategies applicable to handling distributions from employer plans apply to IRAs as well: keep assets in the plan as long as possible, and when transferring IRAs from one investment to another, always arrange for direct rollovers.

However, there is a wrinkle in the IRA rules that can provide an interesting planning opportunity for individuals with short-term cash needs. When you do withdraw IRA assets, you are allowed up to 60 days to re-deposit them free of tax. During that period, you pretty much can do whatever you want with the money.

ILLUSTRATION

It's April 15th, and your taxes are due. You owe $5,000 but don't have the cash. You know your employer will be issuing you a $12,000 bonus on May 1st. You could withdraw the $5,000 from your IRA to pay your taxes, and then redeposit the amount withdrawn when your bonus check comes in.

There are two critical restrictions on your ability to use this strategy. First, you can only take advantage of it once every 12 months. (That's every 12 months, not every year; if you use this technique on May 1, 19X1, you can't use it again in 19X2 until May 2nd.) Second, the law requires you to re-deposit the entire amount withdrawn within 60 days. (That's 60 days, not two months; beware of months with 31 days in them!) Nevertheless, used judiciously, this strategy can help solve short-term cash flow problems in certain circumstances.

Annuitized Distributions

The exception to the 10-percent premature distribution penalty for "annuitized" distributions ("a series of substantially equal periodic payments," in tax jargon) provides an interesting planning opportunity in a small number of cases.

You are 45 years old with $360,000 in IRAs, thanks in part to a rollover from an old employer's plan. According to IRS tables, your life expectancy is 36 years. You can withdraw $10,000 from your account each year without being subject to the 10 percent penalty.

There are a few things to note with this planning strategy. First, it usually will only make sense for people hoping to retire a few years early, and who have large balances in their IRAs; lop a zero off the figures in the last illustration, and you won't be able to do very much with your withdrawals. Next, once you start with this strategy, you *must* continue it until you reach $59\frac{1}{2}$ or for five years, whichever is longer. Also, remember that even though this strategy avoids the 10-percent penalty tax, regular income taxes still are due. Finally, remember that using this strategy causes you to start tapping into retirement savings 10 to 20 years ahead of schedule; review the worksheet from chapter 5 to be certain you will have adequate retirement savings.

Despite these concerns, this strategy can be a nice way to supplement income, retire early, or even other expand financial goals.

Minimum Required Distributions

Except in the case of Roth IRAs, you must begin receiving distributions from retirement accounts shortly after you turn $70\frac{1}{2}$. For people who don't really need the money, but also want to avoid the 50-percent penalty tax for failing to make a required minimum distribution, there is a way to minimize the amount of the required distribution. By naming a beneficiary on the account (which you should have done anyway) you can decrease slightly the amount of the required distribution.

ILLUSTRATION

You are 65 and your partner is 62. Your life expectancy is 15 years, but your joint life expectancy is 18 years. You have $180,000 in an IRA. If you used only your own life expectancy to compute your required minimum distribution, you would have to withdraw and pay taxes on $12,000. However, if you name your partner as your IRA beneficiary and use your joint life expectancy, you would only have to withdraw and pay taxes on $10,000.

This strategy is well-suited to lesbian and gay couples, who may be able to take advantage of an age difference to save taxes on minimum distributions. However, there is a 10-year cut-off on the age difference the IRS life expectancy tables will accommodate; IRS tables will treat your beneficiary as being a maximum of ten years younger than you, even if he or she is much younger.

PART VII

Incapacity Planning

CHAPTER 19

Financial Decision-Making

I f you were to become incapacitated, who would take care of life's everyday tasks for you? The mail still needs to be opened, bills still need to be paid, and doctors need to be told what to do; in short, life would go on. Unless you have designated someone in advance to handle matters like these for you, the person who by law would step in may not know what needs to be done. Normally, that person is a spouse if you are married or a family member if you are single. Partners in gay relationships are not legally recognized for this purpose, even though they may be the most familiar with your wishes and the most appropriate to speak for you.

Unless you want emotionally or geographically distant relatives managing your affairs, perhaps even to the exclusion of your partner, you'll need several legal documents spelling out who is in charge and what you want done. You'll also need to plan separately for financial decision-making and medical decision-making. The former is discussed in this chapter and the latter in the next chapter.

A *general power of attorney* (a "power") authorizes another person (your *attorney-in-fact*) to act on your behalf in financial and business matters in the event you are unable to do so. If you become incapacitated, your attorney-in-fact will need to be able to access your bank and brokerage accounts, make your house or car payments, deal with insurance companies, and generally do all the others things you would do to run your financial life. Because he or she needs this broad grant of authority, it's important that you choose your attorney-in-fact with care. If he or she can access your bank account, he or she also can close it out. If you are in a relationship, you likely trust your partner to handle these things for you. If your partner is bad with money or if you are not in a relationship, you might consider asking a friend or trusted advisor to serve as your attorney-in-fact.

Because the powers you grant to your attorney-in-fact are so comprehensive, you should give some thought as to whether you want those powers to be effective immediately upon executing the document, or not until you are incompetent. The latter are known as *springing powers*, because they "spring" into effect when you become incapacitated. Springing powers offer a little more protection against misuse, but they also mean your incapacity has to be certified before they can be used. Because lesbian and gay couples generally look on powers of attorney as one of the tools they can use to replicate marriage rights, they generally do not need springing powers.

Make sure your power of attorney states that you intend for it to be *durable*—that is, to survive your incapacity. Historically, powers of attorney were not durable, so their modern use for incapacity planning requires you to specify your intentions. Also be sure to execute your power of attorney in accordance with your state's legal requirements. These execution formalities usually cover witness and/or notarization procedures.

The figure below contains a sample general power of attorney. It is provided only to assist you in understanding what powers look like and how they work. Because the laws affecting powers of attorney vary from state to state, you are strongly advised to seek competent legal assistance before executing this or any legal document. Also because of the variety of state laws, your power of attorney may look different than this sample.

FIGURE 19-1
SAMPLE GENERAL POWER OF ATTORNEY

DURABLE GENERAL POWER OF ATTORNEY

* * * * * *

WARNING TO PERSON EXECUTING THIS DOCUMENT:

This is an important legal document. It creates a Durable Power of Attorney. Before you execute this document, you should know these facts:

continues

(continued)

I. This document may provide the person you designate as your attorney-in-fact with broad powers to dispose, sell, convey, and encumber your real and personal property.

2. These powers will exist for an indefinite period of time unless you limit their duration in this document. These powers will continue to exist notwithstanding your subsequent disability or incapacity.

3. You have the right to revoke or terminate this Durable Power of Attorney at any time.

If you do not understand anything in this document, you should seek professional legal advice before signing it.

* * * * * *

To my family, relatives, and friends;

To any person who may have any interest or duty in affairs relating to my finances or property;

To any person who may have any interest or duty in the disposition of my body upon my death; and,

To any other person who may have any interest or duty in the matters contained herein:

1. Creation of Durable Power of Attorney

   I, Susie Sample, being of sound mind and body, willfully and voluntarily intend to create by this document a Durable Power of Attorney by appointing the person designated herein as my attorney-in-fact to make decisions for me in the event I become incapacitated and am unable to make such decisions and take such actions for myself. This Durable Power of Attorney shall not be affected by my subsequent incapacity.

2. Appointment of Attorney-in-Fact

   I hereby appoint Polly Pureheart, currently residing at 123 Memory Lane, Love City, State of Bliss 96969 (telephone 101-555-1234), as my attorney-in-fact, to act for me and in my name, and for my use and benefit, in preference over my blood relatives.

3. When Effective

   This Durable Power of Attorney shall become effective upon its execution.

4. Appointment of Guardian

   My attorney-in-fact is to be appointed guardian of my person and property if I am physically or mentally incapacitated and unable to care for my person or property, in preference over my blood relatives.

5. Financial Matters

   My attorney-in-fact is to have full power and authority over all my property, real, personal, and intangible, and is authorized to do and perform all and every act which I, as owner of the property, could do or perform, in preference over my blood relatives. I hereby ratify and confirm all that my attorney-in-fact shall do or cause to be done under this Durable Power of Attorney.

   The authority of my attorney-in-fact includes, but is not limited to, the authority to:

   (1) Manage my personal finances and property so as to meet any obligations;

continues

(continued)

(2) Deposit into my accounts in any bank, savings and loan, money market, mutual fund or other investment account, or other account of whatsoever type and wheresoever situated of all money that may come to him or her as my attorney-in-fact, and endorse for deposit all such checks or drafts;

(3) Draw checks or drafts on my accounts to meet my financial obligations or maintain funds in any joint account for the payment of any joint expenses;

(4) Purchase or redeem stock, bonds, certificates of deposit, and any other investment security of whatsoever type and wheresoever situated;

(5) Vote shares of stock on my behalf;

(6) Execute and deliver to the proper authorities any documents and remittances that may be necessary to continue proper registration of any motor vehicle in which I have an ownership interest, or sell such vehicle if necessary;

(7) Sell, purchase, or manage real estate in my name and for my benefit, and sign all documents necessary for such transactions;

(8) Represent my interests before insurance companies, employers, or government entities in procuring any insurance, retirement, medical or other benefits to which I may be entitled;

(9) Access any safe deposit box in my name;

(10) Deal with retirement plans including individual retirement accounts, rollovers, and voluntary contributions, change the ownership or beneficiary designations on such accounts, plans, and/or annuities;

(11) Forgive and collect debts;

(12) Make statutory elections and disclaimers, including disclaiming any inheritance or life insurance proceeds or abandoning property interests;

(13) Hire attorneys, accountants, investment advisors, custodians, brokers, agents, and other professionals;

(14) Pursue, settle, or appeal litigation on my behalf;

(15) Sign or amend tax returns or Internal Revenue Service powers of attorney, and settle tax disputes;

(16) Make contributions to charities recognized as such under Section 501 (c)(3) of the Internal Revenue Code;

(17) Make gifts of cash or other property as my attorney-in-fact may in his or her absolute discretion deem appropriate, provided that such gifts are within the dollar limit and made in the manner described by the Internal Revenue Code as qualifying for the gift tax annual exclusion, and further provided that in no circumstances shall any such gift be made for the benefit of my attorney-in-fact, the creditors of my attorney-in-fact, the estate of my attorney-in-fact, or the creditors of the estate of my attorney-in-fact; and,

(18) Fund inter vivos trusts.

continues

(continued)

6. Legal Matters

   My attorney-in-fact is to have all authority to manage any and all legal proceedings for or against me during the period of my incapacity, in preference over my blood relatives, including, but not limited to, the authority to initiate and pursue to final resolution legal action in my name as my attorney-in-fact deems necessary, whether for injunctive, declaratory, compensatory, and/or punitive relief, at the expense of my estate, for any cause of action arising during my incapacity.

7. Reliance by Third Parties

   The powers conferred on my attorney-in-fact by this Durable Power of Attorney may be exercised by my attorney-in-fact alone, and my attorney-in-fact's signature may be accepted by any third person or organization as fully authorized by me and with the same force and effect as if I were personally present, competent, and acting on my own behalf.

   No person or organization who relies on this Durable Power of Attorney or any representation my attorney-in-fact makes regarding his or her authority, including, but not limited to, the fact that this instrument has not been revoked, the fact that I was competent to execute this Durable Power of Attorney, or his or her authority under this Durable Power of Attorney, shall incur any liability to me, my estate, heirs, successors, or assigns because of such reliance.

8. Duration

   This Durable Power of Attorney shall not terminate in the event of my disability or incapacity.

9. Severability

   In the event any provision or provisions of this Durable Power of Attorney are determined to be invalid, the unaffected provisions shall remain in full force and effect.

10. Construction

    This instrument is intended to serve as a General Power of Attorney and, unless and to the extent not inconsistent with a specific provision contained herein, should be interpreted and enforced as such.

11. Signature of Attorney-in-Fact

I certify that this is the signature of my attorney-in-fact:

_____

Polly Pureheart

12. Execution

Executed this ___ day of _____, 199_ at Love City, State of Bliss.

_____

Susie Sample
123 Memory Lane
Love City, State of Bliss 96969

continues

(continued)

Witness: _____

_____

_____

_____

Witness: _____

_____

_____

_____

NOTARIZATION

CITY OF LOVE   )

)   ss:

STATE OF BLISS   )

I HEREBY CERTIFY THAT, on this ___ day of _____, 199_, before me, the subscriber, a Notary Public of the State of Bliss personally appeared Susie Sample, personally known to me (or proved to me on the basis of satisfactory evidence) to be the person whose name is subscribed to in this instrument, a Durable General Power of Attorney, and acknowledged that she executed it.

I declare under penalty of perjury that the person whose name is subscribed to this instrument appears to be of sound mind and body and under no duress, fraud, or undue influence.

As WITNESS my hand and Notarial Seal.

_____

Notary Public

My Commission Expires: _____

There is one important challenge facing lesbians and gay men who include powers of attorney in their incapacity planning: when your attorney-in-fact tries to use it, he or she may encounter difficulties. Banks, for example, are notorious for requiring that you use "their form" to create a power of attorney. This usually occurs because third parties are afraid of being sued if something goes wrong.

There are steps you can take to minimize potential problems down the road. Your power of attorney should include language stating that you will "hold harmless" any individual who acts in reliance on the power. This is your promise to third parties who act in good faith that you won't sue them if something goes wrong. Next, include a sample of your attorney-in-fact's signature in the document. The third party then can compare that sample with your attorney-in-fact's actual signature when he or she presents your powers. Also, keep your power of attorney current by periodically executing a new one. A "fresh" power gives greater assurance that it remains valid. Ideally, a power should not be more than five years old. Finally, send copies of your executed powers to all your bankers, brokers, insurance agents, and other financial advisers and ask that they be placed in your file.

If your attorney-in-fact does encounter problems in having your power of attorney honored by a financial institution, he or she should be certain management has been consulted. Often, front-line employees simply are not given the authority to act in reliance on powers in an unfamiliar format. It never hurts to ask to speak to a supervisor, or even to ask a supervisor to consult with the institution's legal department.

You can revoke your power of attorney at any time. Simply destroy the original and retrieve and destroy all copies. Notify in writing all third parties (bankers, brokers) that you have revoked your power of attorney, and ask them to return their copies to you.

CHAPTER 20

Medical Decision-Making

I n addition to financial matters, lesbians and gay men—and especially lesbian and gay couples—need to include health care decision-making in their incapacity planning. Once again, the legal and health care systems will not recognize your partner or best friend as your surrogate decision-maker unless you prepare in advance for this contingency. The situation is even more complex with respect to health care decisions, however, in part because a broader range of needs must be met, and in part because in many states two separate planning documents have evolved to address those needs.

Most people are familiar with the *health care directive*, popularly known as a "living will." It contains advance written instructions to health care providers outlining the circumstances under which a person does not wish to receive life-sustaining measures, in a format approved by the laws of your state. A different document, a *health care power of attorney* (a "power"), allows you to appoint another person (your *attorney-in-fact*) to make medical decisions for you when you are incapable of making them for yourself. Although health care powers and living wills can work in tandem, they do not serve the same purpose, and you are likely to need both. A few states allow health care powers and living wills to be combined into a single document known as an *advance medical directive*.

HEALTH CARE POWERS OF ATTORNEY

A durable power of attorney for health care works much like the durable general power of attorney discussed in the last chapter: you grant powers to your attorney-in-fact to make health care decisions in the event of your incapacity. The same rules on durability, execution, acceptance, and revocation apply here. Once again, be sure to give your attorney-in-fact broad powers. These powers should include the authority to: consent to treatment; refuse treatment; withdraw treatment; act in contradiction to medical advice; discharge any health care provider; and, discharge you from a health care facility. As with financial powers, the more assurances you can provide in the document the more likely you are of having your wishes complied with.

There is one additional power specific to the health care context that every lesbian and gay couple needs: a *priority of visitation*. Legally, your biological family has the right to bar your partner from visiting you in the hospital or other health care facility. A priority of visitation denies them this right, and in fact allows your partner to determine who visits and who does not. The priority of visitation is a critical tool for dealing with stress-induced hostilities, and your health care power of attorney should include it explicitly.

The figure below contains a sample health care power of attorney. It is provided only to assist you in understanding what powers look like and how they work. Because the laws affecting health care decision-making can vary significantly from state to state, you are strongly advised to seek competent legal assistance before executing this or any legal document. Also because of the variety of state laws, your power of attorney may look different than this sample.

FIGURE 20-1
SAMPLE HEALTH CARE POWER OF ATTORNEY

DURABLE POWER OF ATTORNEY FOR HEALTH CARE

* * * * * *

WARNING TO PERSON EXECUTING THIS DOCUMENT:

This is an important legal document. It creates a Durable Power of Attorney. Before you execute this document, you should know these facts:

continues

(continued)

1. This document may provide the person you designate as your attorney-in-fact with broad powers to consent to, withhold, or authorize the withdrawal of your medical treatment.

2. These powers will exist for an indefinite period of time unless you limit their duration in this document. These powers will continue to exist notwithstanding your subsequent disability or incapacity.

3. You have the right to revoke or terminate this Durable Power of Attorney at any time.

   If you do not understand anything in this document, you should seek professional legal advice before signing it.

* * * * * *

To my family, relatives, and friends;

To physicians, health care providers, community care facilities, dentists, paramedics, pharmacists, and to any other person who may have any interest or duty in my medical care or treatment;

To any person who may have any interest or duty in the disposition of my body upon my death; and,

To any other person who may have any interest or duty in the matters contained herein:

1. Creation of Durable Power of Attorney

   I, Susie Sample, being of sound mind and body, willfully and voluntarily intend to create by this document a Durable Power of Attorney by appointing the person designated herein as my attorney-in-fact to make decisions for me in the event I become incapacitated and am unable to make such decisions and take such actions for myself. This Durable Power of Attorney shall not be affected by my subsequent incapacity.

2. Appointment of Attorney-in-Fact

   I hereby appoint Polly Pureheart, currently residing at 123 Memory Lane, Love City, State of Bliss 96969 (telephone 101-555-1234), as my attorney-in-fact, to act for me and in my name, and for my use and benefit, in preference over my blood relatives.

3. When Effective

   This Durable Power of Attorney shall become effective in the event I become physically or mentally incapacitated and am unable to make decisions and act for myself, or if I am otherwise unable to handle such medical, legal or financial affairs as are described below.

4. Determination of Incapacity

   The determination that I have become incapacitated and am unable to make decisions for myself shall be made by a licensed physician. This Durable Power of Attorney shall become effective upon written verification of such determination by such licensed physician. Oral verification shall be sufficient to make this Durable Power of Attorney effective in the event of an emergency. If possible, the determination should be made by the doctor who is known to my attorney-in-fact as my preferred current primary physician.

continues

(continued)

5. Medical Matters

My attorney-in-fact shall have full authority to make all health care decisions for me including, but not limited to:

(1) My admission into or discharge from any hospital or other health care facility, with or without medical advice;

(2) Employ or discharge medical personnel responsible for my care; review any and all information contained in my medical records, and to disclose the contents thereof to any or all persons as he or she alone deems appropriate;

(3) Expend or withhold my funds for any medical or similar treatment and determine what claims for benefit may be submitted to any insurer or agency that may be liable for the costs of my care;

(4) Consent or withdraw consent or refuse consent to any care, treatment, service, or procedure to maintain, diagnose, or treat my mental or physical condition including, but not limited to, examinations, performance of tests, surgery, therapies, administration of medication, and the use of mechanical devices including, but not limited to, devices designed to provide artificial respiration, nutrition, or hydration;

(5) Execute on my behalf any and all appropriate documents, including, but not limited to documents titled or purporting to be a "Refusal to Permit Treatment" or "Leaving Hospital Against Medical Advice", and any waiver or release from liability required by a hospital or physician; and,

(6) Initiate and pursue to final resolution legal action in my name as my attorney-in-fact deems necessary, whether for injunctive, declaratory, compensatory, and/or punitive relief, at the expense of my estate, to compel compliance with my wishes, and to seek damages for failure to comply with those wishes.

6. Priority of Visitation

In the event of any injury, illness, incapacity, or incarceration, my attorney-in-fact is to have first priority to visit me in any facility, in preference over my blood relatives, and under no circumstances is he or she to be denied access to me. Further, in the event restrictions are placed on visitations to me, for medical or other reasons, my attorney-in-fact is to have exclusive authority, in preference over my blood relatives, in determining the priority of such visitations and may deny such visitations to any and all persons as he or she alone determines to be in my best interest.

7. Appointment of Guardian

My attorney-in-fact is to be appointed guardian of my person and property if I am physically or mentally incapacitated and unable to care for my person or property, in preference over my blood relatives.

8. Reliance by Third Parties

The powers conferred on my attorney-in-fact by this Durable Power of Attorney may be exercised by my attorney-in-fact alone, and my attorney-in-fact's signature may be accepted by any third person or organization as fully authorized by me and with the same force and effect as if I were personally present, competent, and acting on my own behalf.

continues

(continued)

No person or organization who relies on this Durable Power of Attorney or any representation my attorney-in-fact makes regarding his or her authority, including, but not limited to, the fact that this instrument has not been revoked, the fact that I was competent to execute this Durable Power of Attorney, or his or her authority under this Durable Power of Attorney, shall incur any liability to me, my estate, heirs, successors, or assigns because of such reliance.

9. Duration

I intend that this Durable Power of Attorney remain effective until my death, or until revoked by me in writing.

10. Severability

In the event any provision or provisions of this Durable Power of Attorney are determined to be invalid, the unaffected provisions shall remain in full force and effect.

11. Signature of Attorney-in-Fact

I certify that this is the signature of my attorney-in-fact:

_____

Polly Pureheart

12. Execution

Executed this ___ day of _____, 199X at City of Love, State of Bliss.

_____

Susie Sample

123 Memory Lane

Love City, State of Bliss 96969

Witness:

_____
_____
_____
_____

Witness:

_____
_____
_____
_____

NOTARIZATION

CITY OF LOVE   )
)   ss:
STATE OF BLISS   )

continues

(continued)

I HEREBY CERTIFY THAT, on this ___ day of _____, 199_ before me, the subscriber, a Notary Public of the State of Bliss, personally appeared Susie Sample, personally known to me (or proved to me on the basis of satisfactory evidence) to be the person whose name is subscribed to in this instrument, a Durable Power of Attorney For Health Care, and acknowledged that she executed it.

I declare under penalty of perjury that the person whose name is subscribed to this instrument appears to be of sound mind and body and under no duress, fraud, or undue influence.

As WITNESS my hand and Notarial Seal.

_____
Notary Public

My Commission Expires: _____

LIVING WILLS

In contrast to a health care power of attorney, a living will directs your health care providers not to prolong your life through the use of artificial means in the event you become terminally or incurably ill, or lapse into a "chronic vegetative state." Your living will should spell out what procedures you want withheld and the circumstances under which to do so. Typically, these include artificial respiration or ventilation, heart pumps, dialysis, and the administration of food and water. Be sure to list specific medical procedures you want withheld that otherwise would be administered to you. Be warned, however: what you can and cannot include in a living will varies by state. It's critical that you follow the rules in your state explicitly, or your living will may not be valid. The figure below contains a sample living will. You can use it to understand the basics of how these documents work, but it's best to get professional advice on the laws in your state.

FIGURE 20-2
SAMPLE HEALTH CARE DECLARATION

HEALTH CARE DECLARATION

On this ___ day of _____, 199_, I, SUSIE SAMPLE, being of sound mind, willfully and voluntarily direct that my dying shall not be artificially prolonged under the circumstances set forth in this Declaration:

continues

(continued)

If at any time I should have an incurable injury, disease, or illness certified to be a terminal condition by two (2) physicians who have personally examined me, one (1) of whom shall be my attending physician, and the physicians have determined that my death is imminent and will occur whether or not life-sustaining procedures are utilized and where the application of such procedures would serve only to prolong artificially the dying process, I direct that such procedures be withheld or withdrawn, and that I be permitted to die naturally with only the administration of medication, the administration of food and water without use of artificial or mechanical means, and the performance of any medical procedure that is necessary to provide comfort, care, or alleviate pain. In the absence of my ability to give directions regarding the use of such life-sustaining procedures, it is my intention that this Declaration shall be honored by my family, attorney(s)-in-fact, and health care provider(s) as the final expression of my right to control my medical care and treatment.

I am legally competent to make this Declaration, and I understand its full import.

Signed _____

SUSIE SAMPLE
123 Memory Lane
Love City, State of Bliss 96969

Under penalty of perjury, we state that this Declaration was signed by SUSIE SAMPLE in the presence of the undersigned who, at her request, in her presence, and in the presence of each other, have hereunto signed our names as witnesses this ___ day of _____, 199_. Further, each of us, individually, states that: the Declarant is known to me, and I believe the Declarant to be of sound mind. I did not sign the Declarant's signature to this Declaration. Based upon information and belief, I am not related to the Declarant by blood or marriage, a creditor of the Declarant, entitled to any portion of the estate of the Declarant under any existing testamentary instrument of the Declarant, entitled to any financial benefit by reason of the death of the Declarant, financially or otherwise responsible for the Declarant's medical care, nor an employee of any such person or institution.

_____

_____

_____

_____

_____

_____

_____

_____

CITY OF LOVE   )

) ss:

STATE OF BLISS   )

continues

(continued)

I HEREBY CERTIFY THAT, on this ___ day of _____, 199_, before me, the subscriber, a Notary Public of the State of Bliss, personally appeared SUSIE SAMPLE, Declarant, and _____, and _____, Witnesses, and acknowledged the foregoing document to be their act.

As WITNESS my hand and Notarial Seal.

_____
Notary Public

My Commission Expires: _____

What's the difference between a living will and a health care power of attorney? A living will only applies in situations where your death is inevitable; it has no relevance to any other type of incapacity. Also, there's a chance your doctors may not honor your living will (they may decide death is not inevitable, living wills may be only "advisory" in your state). In such a circumstance, the health care power would give your attorney-in-fact the authority to enforce the preferences you expressed through your living will. Again, unless you live in a state that's combined living wills and health care powers into a single advance medical directive, you need both documents to adequately complete your incapacity planning.

As with financial powers, health care powers and living wills are only as good as the person you present them to thinks they are. The same advice given in the last chapter for your powers applies here.

FIGURE 20-3
CHECKLIST FOR POWERS OF ATTORNEY

Taking the following steps should insure that your power of attorney is respected by third parties when it is presented to them:

_____ Send copies of your power of attorney and your living will to all your health care professionals, and ask them to place the copy in your file. (Similarly, send copies of your general power of attorney to all the your financial professionals.)

_____ Include a priority of visitation in your health care power of attorney.

_____ Include a "hold harmless" clause in all powers of attorney.

_____ Include a sample of your attorney-in-fact's signature in all powers of attorney.

_____ Keep your powers of attorney "current"; try not to let the date of execution get more than five years old.

_____ Always speak to supervisory personnel at any institution refusing to honor a power of attorney.

PART VIII

Getting Help

CHAPTER 21

Choosing a Trustee or Executor

Estate and incapacity planning require you to name other people to make decisions for you when you are no longer able to make them yourself. As you learned in earlier chapters, this person is a *trustee* (or co-trustee) in the case of a trust; an *executor* (also known as a personal representative or administrator, depending on your state) for a will; and, an *attorney-in-fact* for a power of attorney. Although the titles change, the roles and responsibilities are quite similar: to carry out your wishes in responsibly managing your property (or your health care). The law refers to a person given this responsibility as a *fiduciary*.

Deciding whom to trust with this responsibility is no small matter, although most people don't give it the thought that it deserves. If you are in a relationship, you're likely to name your partner as your fiduciary. Usually this is a good choice, but you should read on for some additional considerations. If you're not in a relationship, or if your partner lacks aptitude or interest in managing money, you'll need to find someone else to serve. Family members or friends also are common choices to serve as fiduciaries, but the above-mentioned problems with ability and willingness to serve still apply. Moreover, for gay people, isolation from family members may preclude choosing them as fiduciaries. Finally, if you have a substantial net worth, it may not be very prudent to rely on anybody close to you—partner, family, or friends—to manage your assets.

In any of these circumstances, you may need to consider using a professional as a fiduciary. This can be either an individual (attorney, accountant) or an institution (bank, trust company). There are some important points to bear in mind if you go this route:

1. The fiduciary will charge a fee for his or her services. You should understand this fee in advance; in some cases the fees professional fiduciaries charge can be substantial, and they will consume a small portion of your assets.

2. Because institutional fiduciaries tend to be very large organizations, you may not be able to know in advance with whom your beneficiaries will be dealing. There have been instances in which even seemingly gay-friendly institutions have treated surviving partners inappropriately.

3. Institutional fiduciaries tend to be very cautious in managerial decision-making out of (justifiable) fear of being sued by disgruntled beneficiaries.

What can you do to avoid or minimize potential problems that can arise through the use of professional fiduciaries? Here are a few possibilities to consider:

1. If it's a close call as to whether or not to name a loved one or a professional to serve as your fiduciary, you could name the former and include provisions in your documents authorizing him or her to engage the services of the latter.

2. If the need for a professional fiduciary is clear, consider your current advisors first. If they're willing to serve, they may be more cost-effective and sensitive to your needs. Accountants are an excellent but often-overlooked alternative on both counts.

3. If you do choose an institutional fiduciary, be sure you also name a *trust protector* in your document. This person, who should be disinterested but known to your beneficiaries, is granted the limited power to replace one institutional fiduciary with another in the event the parties involved cannot work together. Your current advisors all are excellent candidates to serve in this role.

A final point about fiduciaries: it's almost always a good idea to name an alternate fiduciary to serve in case your first choice can't or won't. This is a contingency that can present real problems at the time it comes to pass, so it is best planned for in advance.

Regardless of whether you use a partner, friend, family member, or professional fiduciary, be sure you've chosen the person who can best manage your assets. Remember, this is not a popularity contest—besides, there are better ways to use a will or trust to tell people what you think of them!

CHAPTER 22

Choosing an Advisor

A lthough this book has been designed to provide a great deal of practical advice and hands-on tools to help members of the lesbian and gay community, there are times when you're simply ill-advised to take a do-it-yourself approach. Many of the decisions you'll need to make as you work through the financial planning process carry high price tags if you misapply the rules you've learned here.

When you're faced with an important financial planning decision, you should always consider calling in professional assistance. This would be easier to do if you knew who to look for and what to ask. This chapter can help you sort out the various types of financial planning professionals, the unique skills they have, and the questions you need to ask in order to be sure you've found the right person for the job.

TYPES OF FINANCIAL PLANNING PROFESSIONALS

People come to the financial planning profession from a wide variety of backgrounds—law, accounting, insurance, investments, and so on. In order to know whether you've identified a potential planner suited to your needs, you should understand the titles that go with these various backgrounds. The table below contains information to help you distinguish the terms widely used by financial planning professionals to describe themselves, their credentials, and their services.

FIGURE 22-1
TYPES OF FINANCIAL PLANNING PROFESSIONALS

Accredited Business Accountant (ABA). A private credential administered by the Accreditation Council for Accountancy and Taxation (ACAT), ABAs meet examination, continuing education, experience, and ethics requirements. ABAs are subject to disciplinary action by ACAT.

Accredited Tax Preparer (ATP). A private credential administered by the Accreditation Council for Accountancy and Taxation (ACAT), ATPs meet initial examination, continuing education, experience and ethics requirements. ATPs are subject to disciplinary action by ACAT.

Accredited Tax Advisor (ATA). A private credential administered by the Accreditation Council for Accountancy and Taxation (ACAT), ATAs meet comprehensive examination, continuing education, experience, and ethics requirements. ATAs are subject to disciplinary action by ACAT.

Accountant. A generic term used to describe anyone who practices accounting; the regulation of the practice of accountancy varies widely by state. In some states only CPAs can use the term accountant, but in others anyone can. Depending on state law, accountants may or may not be subject to disciplinary action by the state board of accountancy.

Attorney. A member of a state bar. Some attorneys limit their practices to tax or estate planning. In a few states, attorneys are permitted to call themselves specialists if they pass an examination given by the state bar; in others use of the term "specialist" is prohibited. Attorneys are subject to disciplinary action by the state bar. Attorneys also are permitted to represent clients before the Internal Revenue Service.

Certified Financial Planner (CFP). A widely recognized private credential administered by the CFP Board. CFPs meet comprehensive education, examination, experience, continuing education, and ethics requirements. CFPs are subject to disciplinary action by the CFP Board.

Certified Life Underwriter/Chartered Financial Consultant (CLU/ChFC). Private credentials administered by the American College of CLU/ChFCs. CLUs complete an educational program and maintain continuing education in the area of life insurance planning. ChFCs meet education, examination, experience, continuing education, and ethics requirements, also with something of an insurance industry focus. CLU/ChFCs are subject to disciplinary action by the American College.

Certified Public Accountant (CPA). A credential administered by the state board of accountancy. CPAs meet comprehensive examination, continuing education, experience, and ethics requirements. CPAs are subject to disciplinary action by the state board of accountancy. CPAs also are permitted to represent clients before the Internal Revenue Service.

Enrolled Agent (EA). A designation authorized by the Internal Revenue Service (IRS) permitting individuals with demonstrated expertise to represent clients before the agency. EAs meet comprehensive examination, education, experience, and continuing education requirements. EAs are subject to disciplinary action by the IRS.

Estate Planner. A generic term used by a financial planner who limits his or her practice to estate planning. Only licensed attorneys can legally draft estate planning documents. Absent another credential, estate planners are not regulated.

continues

(continued)

Financial Planner. A generic term used by a variety of professionals to describe practices ranging from insurance or investment sales to comprehensive financial planning. Absent another credential, financial planners are largely unregulated, except in a handful of states.

Individual Investment Adviser (IIA). An individual who has satisfied examination requirements imposed by state and federal law and is licensed to sell mutual funds, stocks, and bonds. IIAs work independently of any affiliation with a particular securities brokerage house. IIAs are subject to discipline by the federal or state governmental body with which they are licensed.

Insurance Agent or Broker. Someone licensed to sell insurance products in a state. Agents represent a single insurance company, while brokers work with numerous companies on behalf of their clients. Insurance agents or brokers are subject to disciplinary action by the state insurance commissioner.

Registered Investment Advisor (RIAs). Someone registered with the U.S. Securities and Exchange Commission (SEC) and/or a state securities agency to sell securities (mutual funds, stocks, and bonds), manage assets, and hold themselves out as financial planners. RIAs are subject to disciplinary action by the federal or state governmental body with which they are registered.

Registered Representative. An individual who has satisfied examination requirements imposed by state and federal law and is licensed to sell mutual funds, stocks, and bonds. Registered representatives are affiliated with a single securities brokerage house. They are subject to discipline by the federal or state governmental body with which they are licensed.

Retirement Planner. A generic term used by a financial planner who limits his or her practice to retirement planning. Absent another credential, retirement planners are not regulated.

INTERVIEWING A PLANNER

Finding the right financial planning professional is not always easy. Most people start with referrals from friends or family. If this isn't an option for you, sometimes advertisements in community publications can point you in the right direction. Of course, neither option alone is sufficient; you must interview a potential planner to be certain that he or she can meet your needs, and that you can develop a good working relationship. The table below can help you do that; it contains a list of questions you should ask any planner you're thinking about working with. Some of the questions are general, others specific to a particular financial planning discipline. Use them to help structure your first meeting with a potential planner. (Note that the table assumes you have read this book and are familiar with the concepts underlying each question.)

FIGURE 22-2
SAMPLE QUESTIONS
FOR INTERVIEWING A FINANCIAL PLANNER

GENERAL QUESTIONS

How long have you been in practice?

What is your educational background?

What are your credentials and licenses?

How do you keep current on developments in financial planning?

How are you compensated?

When do you refer clients to other professionals?

What are the names and phone numbers of the other professionals you routinely refer clients to?

What percentage of your clients is gay?

How long have you been serving the lesbian and gay community?

How do you keep current on financial planning developments important to your lesbian and gay clients?

Would you be willing to provide the names and numbers of a few gay or lesbian clients as references?

FOR INSURANCE PLANNING

Do you recommend specific insurance company products?

How are you compensated for your recommendations?

Are you familiar with the "insurable interest" requirements of the life insurers you work with?

How do the property insurers you work with handle homeowners insurance for gay couples?

How do the property insurers you work with handle automobile insurance for gay couples?

FOR INVESTMENT PLANNING

Do you recommend specific investments?

How are you compensated for your recommendations?

Do you have an investment policy statement?

What is your approach to asset allocation?

How often do you recommend clients replace existing investments?

Optional: What are your views on socially-responsible investing?

Optional: How do you monitor the social-issue performance of the investments you recommend?

continues

(continued)

FOR INCOME TAX PLANNING

Do you prepare income tax returns? If so, how many?

How do you help clients minimize their tax bills?

What tax planning strategies do you recommend for your lesbian and gay clients?

FOR RETIREMENT PLANNING

How do you help clients compute their retirement needs?

How do you advise gay couples to plan for retirement?

FOR ESTATE PLANNING

Do you counsel clients to minimize probate? If so, how?

How do you evaluate the federal estate tax exposure of lesbian and gay couples?

What are the inheritance tax rules in our state?

For attorneys: What percentage of your practice is devoted to drafting wills and trusts?

FOR INCAPACITY PLANNING

For attorneys: Do your health care powers of attorney include a priority of visitation clause?

For attorneys: What percentage of your practice is devoted to drafting powers of attorney?

COME OUT

Although there are many things you need to know about a potential planner, there is one important thing he or she is entitled to know about you: your sexual orientation. A fundamental premise of this book is that, while lesbians and gay men share the same financial planning goals as everyone else, the rules and strategies they must employ to achieve those goals are different. The book has taken a fairly comprehensive look at those differences, and by now their importance should be clear to you. It's not very likely your financial planner can be effective in helping you meet your goals unless he or she knows that these different rules and strategies apply to you. You must be completely honest with your planner, and come out at the outset of your relationship.

PART IX

Final Thoughts

CHAPTER 23

Financial Planning Checklist

A lthough originally you may have picked up this book because you had a question about a particular financial planning topic, by now you should have come to appreciate the need for all aspects of financial planning—what professionals refer to as *comprehensive financial planning*. While that term may have slightly different meanings to different people, there is a common set of basic financial planning strategies you should have in place—things every financial planner would review with you if you went to his or her office and asked for a "check-up".

The purpose of this chapter is to help you give yourself just such a check-up. The items contained in the checklist below comprise the basic set of strategies you should have in place—a sort of "minimum daily requirement" of healthy financial planning practices. Your "diet" may require more, but you're guaranteed to need at least this much in order to maintain your fiscal fitness.

Review the list in Figure 23-1 and check off the strategies you've already set in place. Although it may take some time, you'll want to work aggressively to fill in any remaining blanks.

This checklist was designed specifically with lesbians and gay men in mind. While many of the items on it are applicable to all who embrace the financial planning process, some are specifically targeted to the unique needs of the lesbian and gay community.

FIGURE 23-1
BASIC FINANCIAL PLANNING STRATEGIES CHECKLIST

Financial Planning Fundamentals

_____   Prepare a balance sheet and a budget.

_____   Earmark an emergency fund of liquid savings equal to between three and six months of living expenses.

_____   Eliminate all credit card debt.

Investment Planning

_____   Review current portfolio to ensure it is consistent with risk tolerance.

_____   Review current portfolio to ensure proper asset allocation.

_____   Review current portfolio to ensure proper diversification of individual investments.

_____   Review individual investments to ensure adequate performance against benchmark.

_____   Take advantage of dividend reinvestment programs wherever offered.

_____   Adopt a "buy-and-hold" investment strategy; avoid "hot tips" or attempts to "time" the market.

Insurance Planning

_____   Confirm existence and adequacy of current life insurance.

_____   Confirm existence and adequacy of current disability insurance (i.e., replaces 60% to 70% of earnings).

_____   Confirm existence and adequacy of current homeowners or renters insurance.

_____   Confirm existence and adequacy of current auto insurance.

_____   Double-check beneficiary designations on all life insurance policies to confirm they are consistent with your intentions.

continues

(continued)

Income Tax Planning

_____ Review income tax withholding.

_____ Review tax planning strategies chapter of this book to ensure you are taking advantage of all available opportunities.

_____ Make sure you are making maximum allowable contributions to all tax-advantaged retirement plans (401(k)s, IRAs, etc.).

Retirement Planning

_____ Compute monthly savings needs for retirement and begin/increase saving and investing for retirement as needed.

_____ Double-check beneficiary designations on all retirement accounts (401(k)s, IRAs, etc.) to confirm they are consistent with your intentions.

Estate Planning

_____ Consult an estate planner to ensure you have current and adequate wills and will substitutes—this is important for everybody, but critical for lesbian and gay couples.

_____ Determine your need for federal estate tax planning (consider both you and your partner if you are in a relationship).

_____ Determine your need for state inheritance tax planning (consider both you and your partner if you are in a relationship).

_____ Tell at least one family member about the specifics of your estate planning; it may help diffuse conflict later on, especially if you are in a relationship.

Incapacity Planning

_____ Execute a general power of attorney—this is important for everybody, but critical for lesbian and gay couples.

_____ Execute a health care power of attorney, including priority of visitation—this is important for everybody, but critical for lesbian and gay couples.

_____ Execute an advance medical directive (a "living will").

_____ Tell at least one family member about the specifics of your incapacity planning; it may help diffuse conflict later on, especially if you are in a relationship.

CHAPTER 24

Revisiting Your Plan

It's essential to remember that financial planning is a *process*, and not a one-time event. If you want to be sure that your planning is in fact moving you closer to your goals, you need to monitor your progress periodically. One of the most common reasons plans fail is that people don't revisit them.

The checklist in this chapter will help you keep on top of your plan. Topic by topic, it tells you what to do and how often in order to ensure that you're on track to reach your goals.

The checklist is largely self-explanatory, but one quick definition may be helpful. A "life event" refers to a major occurrence in your life that may cause you to alter your goals. Common examples include the birth of a child (your own or a loved one's), the death of a partner or family member, or the beginning or end of a relationship.

FIGURE 24-1
FINANCIAL PLANNING REVIEW CHECKLIST

Once a Year:

_____ *Financial Planning Fundamentals:* Review and update your budget.

_____ *Financial Planning Fundamentals:* Compare current budget and prior budget to track spending, identify opportunities to decrease expenses and increase savings.

_____ *Financial Planning Fundamental:* Review and update your financial statement.

continues

213

(continued)

Once a Year:

_____ *Financial Planning Fundamentals:* Review cash and cash equivalents section of your financial statement to ensure adequacy and availability of emergency fund.

_____ *Financial Planning Fundamentals:* Review liabilities section of your financial statement to ensure progress toward elimination of any consumer debt.

_____ *Investment Planning:* Review individual investment performance; consider replacing individual investments whose three-, five-, or ten-year average return is more than 20% below its benchmark.

_____ *Income Tax Planning:* File all income tax returns.

_____ *Income Tax Planning:* Ensure maximum contributions are being made to all available tax-favored retirement accounts (401(k)s, deductible IRAs and/or Roth IRAs).

_____ *Income Tax Planning:* Donate unneeded clothes and household furnishings to charity (remember to obtain an itemized receipt).

Once Every Two Years:

_____ *Insurance Planning:* Update the personal property inventory you've made to document losses in the event of theft or damage to your home.

_____ *Investment Planning:* Review individual investment performance; consider replacing individual investments whose five- or ten-year average return has run more than 10% below its benchmark over the two-year period.

_____ *Investment Planning:* Review investment portfolio to ensure that asset allocation remains consistent with investment goals; reallocate portfolio as necessary.

Once Every Three Years:

_____ *Insurance Planning:* Review value of use assets on balance sheet to ensure adequacy of existing property insurance coverage.

_____ *Insurance Planning:* Comparison shop automobile insurance premiums; consider changing only if your current insurer's premiums are more than 10% above competitors (most insurers reward customer loyalty).

continues

(continued)

_____ *Investment Planning:* Review individual investment performance; consider replacing individual investments whose ten-year average return has run below its benchmark over the three-year period.

_____ *Investment Planning:* Review the annual in-force policy illustration sent by your insurance company for any cash value insurance you own to compare your policy's actual financial performance with earlier projected results.

_____ *Income Tax Planning:* Review tax planning strategies chapter of this book to ensure you are taking advantage of all applicable opportunities.

_____ *Income Tax Planning:* If you prepare your own income tax return, consider asking a professional to review it for possible tax savings opportunities.

_____ *Retirement Planning:* Recompute monthly retirement savings needs to ensure existing projections remain accurate.

Once Every Five Years:

_____ *Insurance Planning:* Review life insurance needs, and increase or decrease coverage as necessary.

_____ *Estate Planning:* Review net worth on balance sheet to determine need for additional federal estate tax planning or state inheritance tax planning.

_____ *Incapacity Planning:* Consider executing fresh powers of attorney.

Once Every Ten Years:

_____ *Estate Planning:* Review wills and trusts to ensure that beneficiaries, executors, and trustees remain consistent with your intentions.

_____ *Incapacity Planning:* Re-execute all powers of attorney.

After a Life Event:

_____ *Insurance Planning:* Review life insurance needs, and increase or decrease coverage as necessary.

continues

(continued)

After a Life Event:

_____*Insurance Planning:* Review beneficiary designations on all life insurance policies to ensure they remain consistent with your intentions.

_____*Income Tax Planning:* Review income tax filing status, withholding, and exemptions claimed.

_____*Retirement Planning:* Review beneficiary designations on all retirement accounts to ensure they remain consistent with your intentions.

_____*Estate Planning:* Review all wills and trusts to ensure that beneficiaries, executors, and trustees remain consistent with your intentions.

_____*Incapacity Planning:* Review all powers of attorney to ensure that attorney-in-fact designations remain consistent with your intentions.

After Leaving a Job:

_____*Insurance Planning:* If your former employer provided group term life insurance, review adequacy of remaining coverage.

_____*Insurance Planning:* If your former employer provided disability insurance, review the need for individual coverage.

_____*Insurance Planning:* If your former employer provided health insurance, review the need for exercising continuation rights under the federal law known as COBRA.

_____*Income Tax Planning:* Review tax withholding; begin making quarterly estimated payments if necessary.

_____*Retirement Planning:* Determine whether retirement plan assets (e.g., 401(k) account balances) must be removed from employer's plan; if removal is optional, review investment performance to determine whether it is desirable; if removal is desirable, always transfer assets directly into a rollover IRA.

_____*Retirement Planning:* Re-compute monthly retirement savings needs to determine impact of job loss (i.e., loss of ability to contribute to 401(k) plan, loss of employer pension, profit-sharing plan, or retirement savings matching plan); increase monthly retirement saving as needed.

Index